New Perspectives:
New Country Houses

Edition 2007

Author: Carles Broto
Publisher: Arian Mostaedi
Editorial Coordinator: Julie Romero, Cristina Soler
Graphic Design: Oriol Vallès
Texts: Contributed by architects

© Carles Broto i Comerma
Jonqueres 10. 1-5.
08003 Barcelona. Spain
tel: +34 93 301 21 99
fax: + 34 93 301 00 21
E-mail: info@linksbooks.net
www.linksbooks.net

All rights reserved. No part of this book may be used or reproduced in any manner whatsoever without written permission except in the case of brief quotations embodied in critical articles and reviews.

New Perspectives:
New Country Houses

Indice

8 **Lucien Colin & Dominique Henriet.** *House in Nancy*

18 **Alvaro Siza.** *Figueiredo House*

26 **Rob Dubois & Shuichi Kobari.** *Sasaki-Tei*

38 **Bart Prince.** *Hight Residence*

50 **Bart Prince.** *Gradow Family Residence*

60 **Harry Seidler & Associati.** *Farrell House*

74 **Shin Takamatsu & Associati.** *Iwai House*

84 **Tadao Ando.** *Lee House*

94 **Eduardo Souto de Moura.** *Baião House*

102 **Eduardo Souto de Moura.** *Bom Jesus House*

110 **Daniele Marques & Bruno Zurkirchen.** *Kraan Lang House*

118 **Behnisch & Partner.** *Charlotte House*

128 **Log Id.** Residential Building in the Black Forest

136 **Mario Botta.** House in Daro-Bellinzona

144 **Eduard Bru.** Cabani House

154 **Daniel Calatayud.** Calatayud House

168 **Per Line.** House in Bryne

178 **Göran Westman GWSK Arkitekter.** Nyström House

188 **Philippe Rotthier & Atlante.** La Maison du Bourgmestre

198 **Elie Mouyal.** Maison Defourcault

210 **Legorreta Arquitectos.** Akle House

218 **Legorreta Arquitectos.** Valle Bravo House

232 **Maurice & Enrico Cerasi.** Villazzi House

244 **Michael Graves.** Graves Residence: The Warehouse

Introduction

Each period in history inscribes into its architecture, in its own particular way, the nature of the relationship between public and private life. This relationship is also expressed with great diversity according to geographical differences. Today, the collective urban utopias of the modern movement have been abandoned, leaving in their wake towers and apartment blocks as the dark symbols of intensive development gone wrong. And although there is a renewed interest in cities through the rehabilitation of historic city centers, the detached single-family house is still the most powerful emblem of our society's ideal and the dream of a happy life.

For an architect, constructing the architectural framework of private space is a strange and evocative process, an experience related to the labyrinths of psychology. How will the respective identities of the client and the architect be combined? Is the dwelling a reflection of the soul of its inhabitants? Or, as Vicente Verdú states, is it "by parts a choice and a penance; an exercise in power and servitude; a face and a mask"? What is important in a house: its appearance? inhabiting it?

Many different points of view on the relationship of buildings to the environment are presented here. Some architects seek fusion and identification with the landscape, as in the Baiâo house in Portugal. Others prefer forceful opposition to the external world, either to create order in nature, as in the Daro house in Switzerland, or to mitigate the disorder of other men, as in the concrete shell of the Iwai house in Kyoto.

It is impossible to review all the different positions on the integration of architecture into the landscape that are expressed within these pages, but it is clear that environmental issues cannot be ignored today. The orientation of a building and calculation of the maximum use of sunlight are recurring themes in the book. In some designs a concern for ecology leads to the use of innovative construction techniques, such as in the Charlotte house, but innovation does not mean erasing or forgetting the past.

The most stimulating part of this project for us was the attempt to publish an open work, with a great wealth of opinion, and to reflect the complexity of contemporary reality with its multiplicity of often contradictory experiences.

Lucien Colin & Dominique Henriet

House in Nancy

Nancy, France

Photographs: Jean-Marie Monthiers, Dominique Henriet

The design of this single-family dwelling in Nancy responds to a basic factor: the adaptation of the building to the physical characteristics of the site, and therefore to the landscape. Located in a residential district, the trapezoid-shaped plot has a steep slope of almost 14 feet that ensures privacy. It is set between two streets, Rue de la Côte and Rue Marquette.

The solution adopted was the creation of two volumes whose orientation was dictated by the situation of the streets: a body set southeast to northwest along Rue Marquette and a body aligned with Rue de la Côte with a north-south orientation. The project is defined by the intersection of these two volumes and the solution of their facades. The first is a parallelepiped that houses the entrance, which is on the southeast facade, giving access to the house by means of a service staircase. A white steel gate protects the property and provides access to the underground garage. The second is a cubic volume that has a greater physical and visual relation to the exterior.

The southeast street-facing facade is characterized by its hermetic appearance, its only window being a narrow glazed horizontal strip. However, the facades defined by the intersection between the two volumes have a more open design, which is suited to their relation to the exterior spaces. This volumetric arrangement serves to ensure privacy and to establish a close relation between the interior program and the swimming pool and garden facilities. The south facade is protected by a brise-soleil in white steel and natural wood.

The interior program is distributed between two floors according to the oblique encounter between the two volumes. Rather than creating residual spaces, this perfectly structures the internal communications and makes full use of the natural light and views.

Ground floor plan

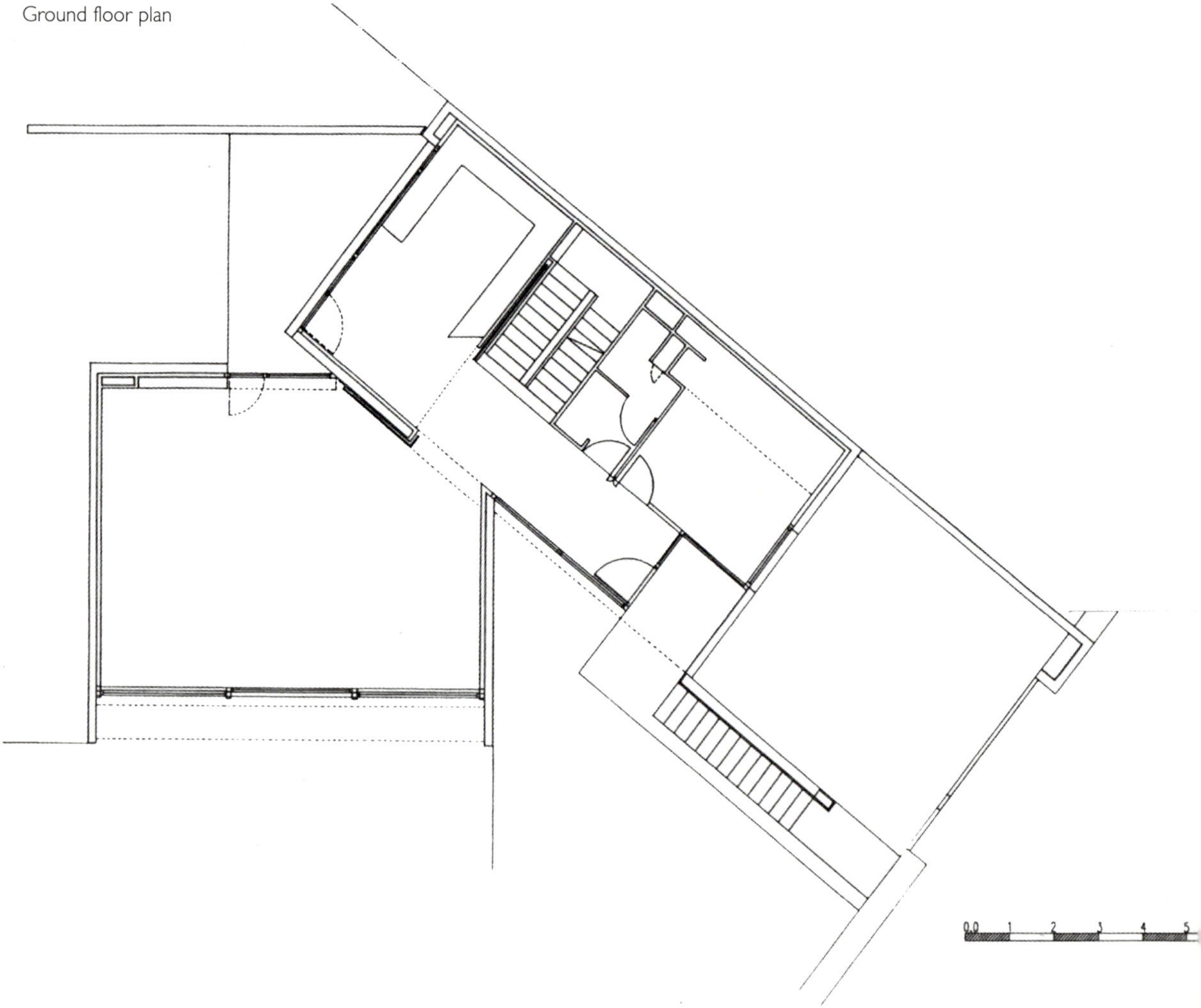

First floor plan

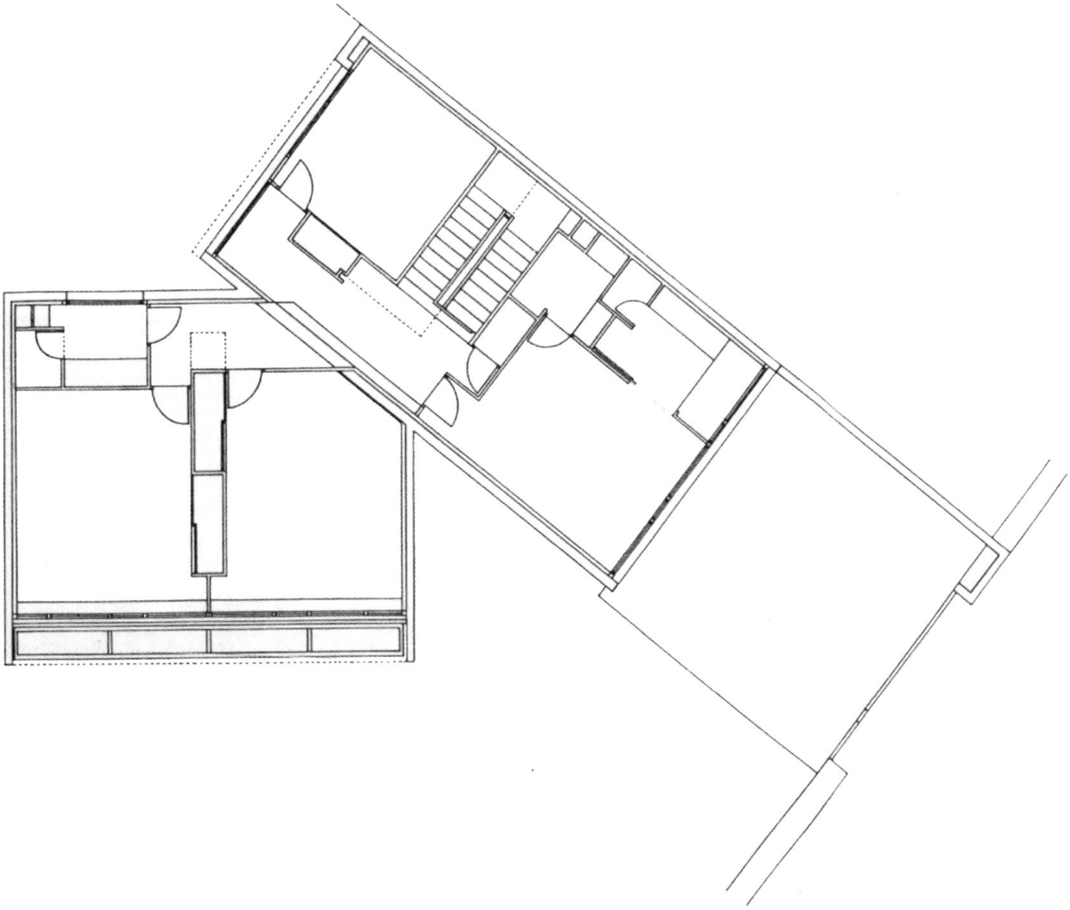

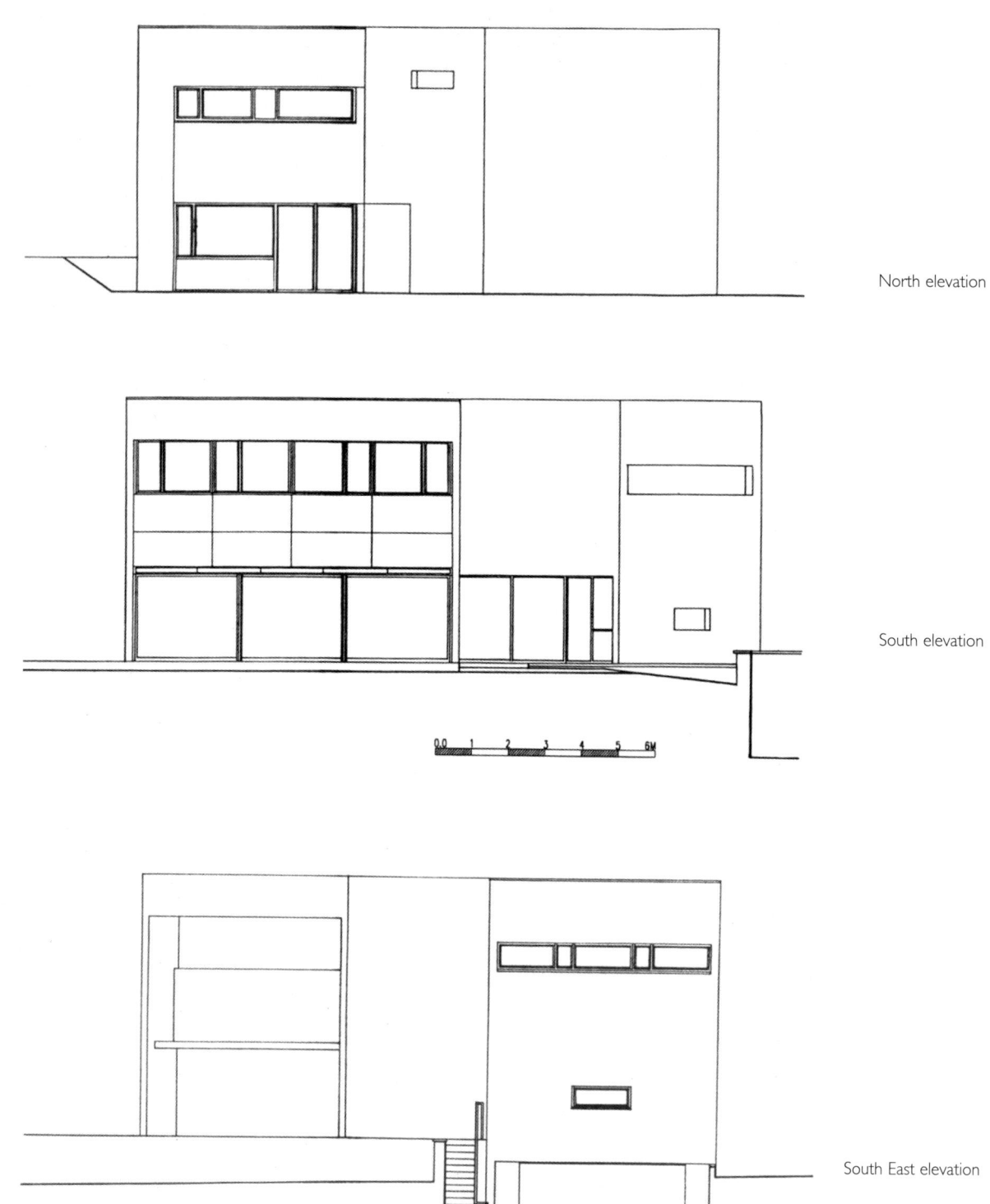

North elevation

South elevation

South East elevation

Alvaro Siza

Figueiredo House

Valbom-Gondomar, Portugal

Photographs: Juan Rodríguez

Figueiredo House, in Valbom-Gondomar, is an excellent example of Alvaro Siza's mastery in composing volumes and geometries of great simplicity. The architect's skill lies in the way that he fits them together, creating new forms and physical relations that enhance the quality of the interior spaces and the development of the visual perspectives of the exterior.

This dwelling is located on a small level plot on one side of the valley where the River Douro crosses the plain on reaching the city of Oporto. It is arranged on two levels in a symmetric composition based on the intersection of two simple figures: a rectangle, where the greater part of the layout is developed, and an octagon, which establishes a basic structural difference between the two floors.

The ground floor is ordered by the axis of the corridor, around which various rooms are distributed. Here, the upper level octagon can only be discerned by the support columns. The building extends in the form of a ship's prow, opened toward the landscape through ample windows.

The octagon plays a dominant role on the upper level. The bedrooms gravitate toward it and the volumetric imbalance that it creates between the levels allowed for a terrace facing the gentle landscape of the valley.

The difference in volumes is also reflected in the facades in the complimentary contrast between the curvature on the lower level and the more severe geometry of the upper level. Nevertheless, the uniform white and the modulation of openings unify the building. Finally, a porch extends from the body of the annex to the entrance of the house.

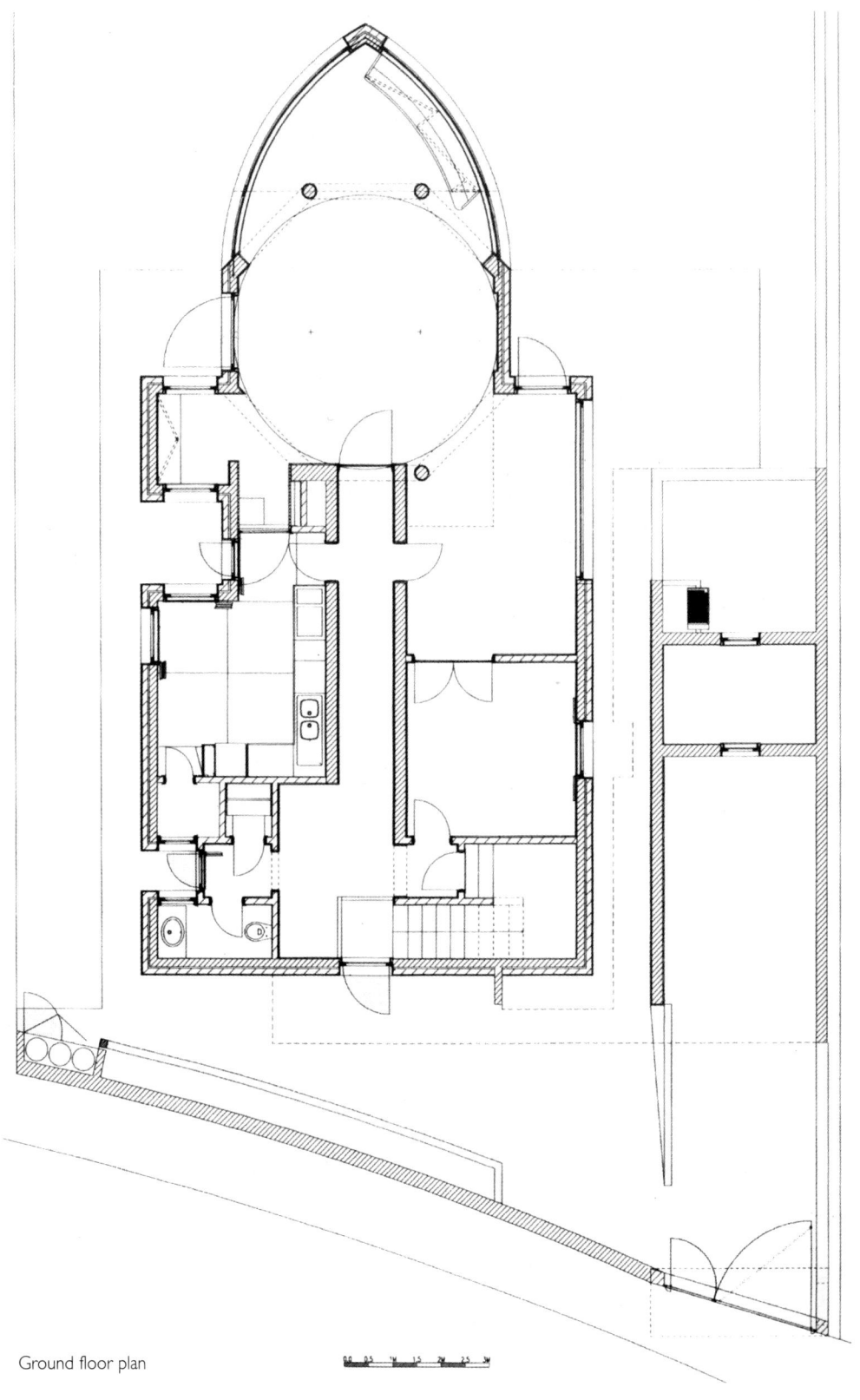

Ground floor plan

First floor plan

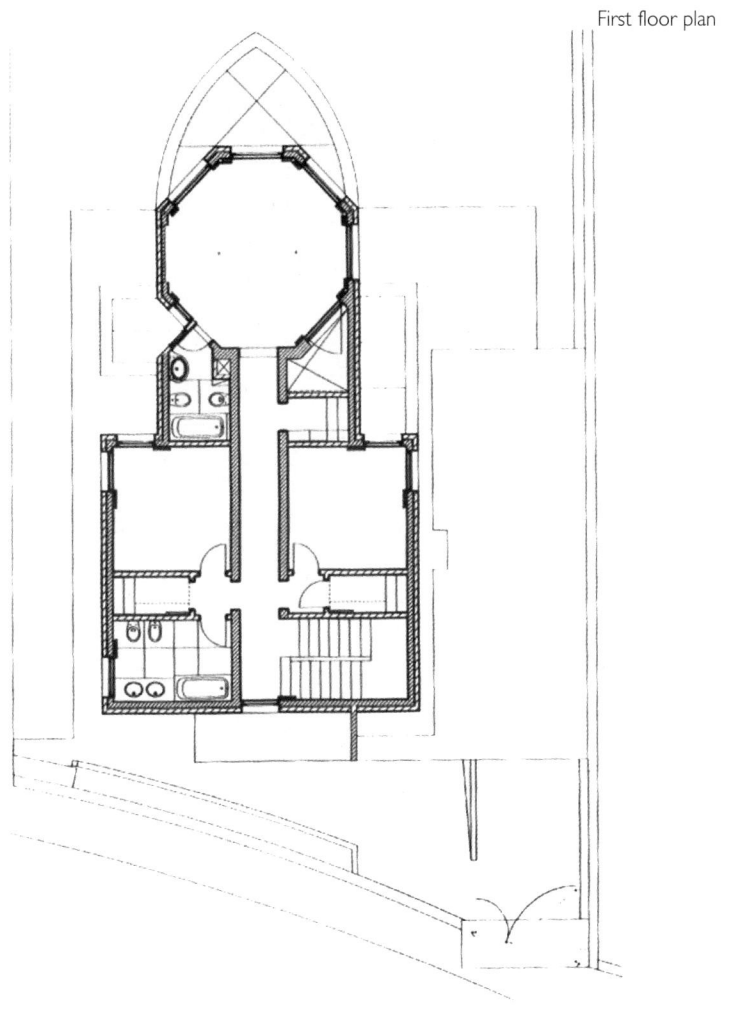

The plastic quality of the interior confirms the expressive role of the solution: the curved glass of the large, visually unobstructed windows allows a panoramic view of the river and landscape. Parquet flooring subtly adds life to the overall design.

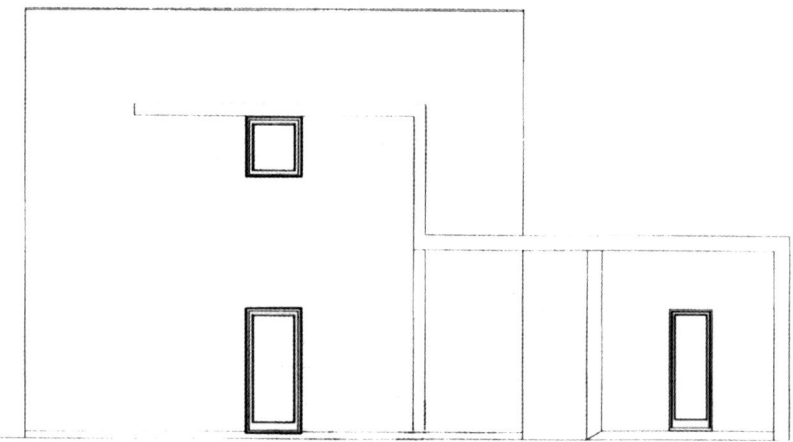

North East elevation

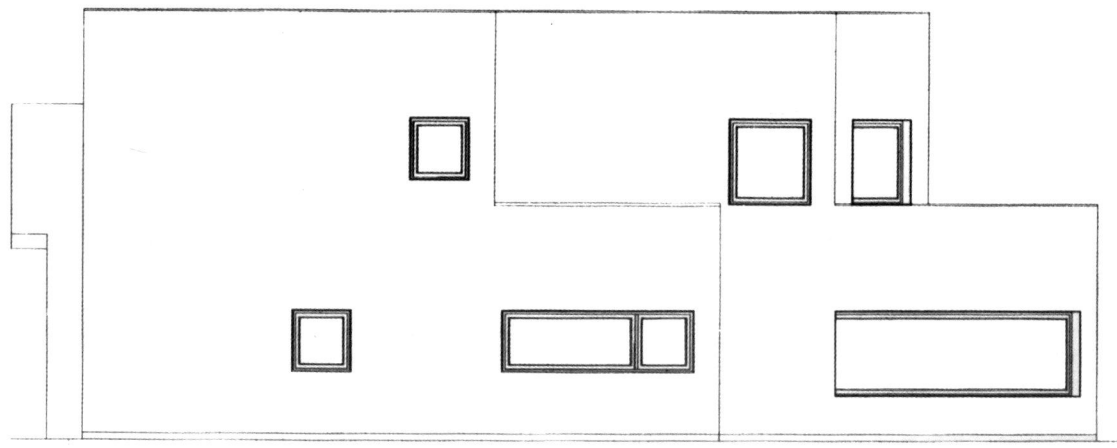

North West elevation

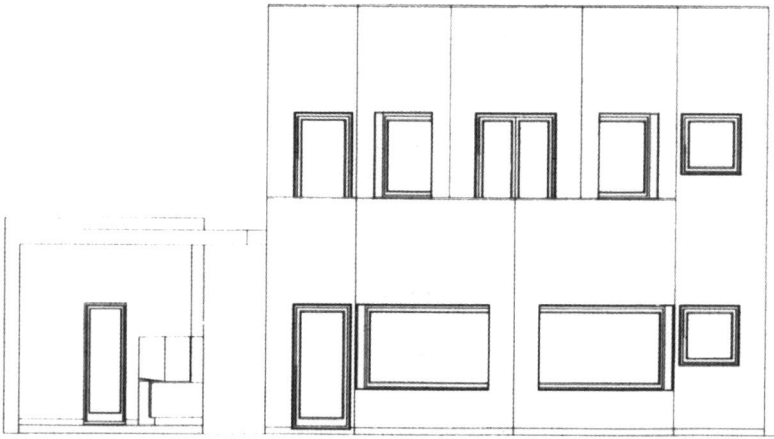

South West elevation

The design of the facades faithfully follows the tradition of rationalism.

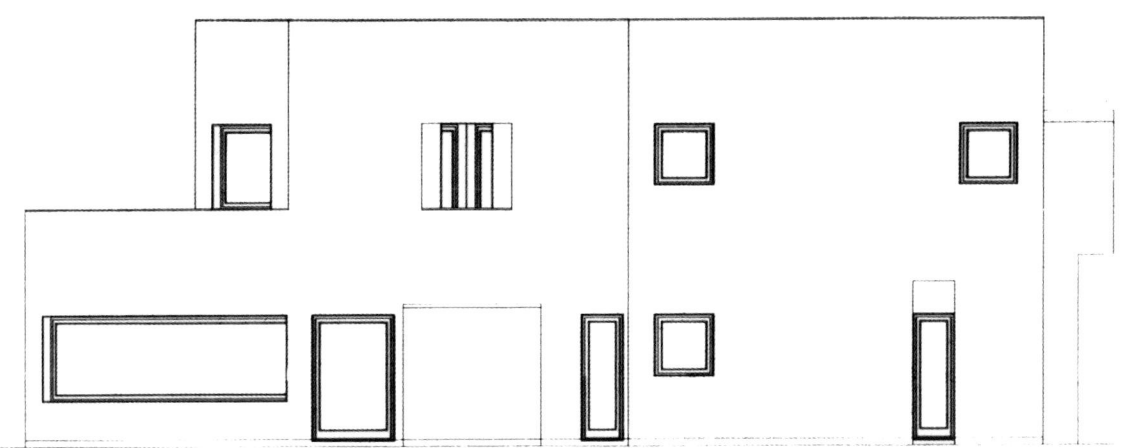

South East elevation

The central motif of the relation between building and site resides in the plastic way in which the building evokes the prow of a ship being steered toward the River Douro from the lawn.

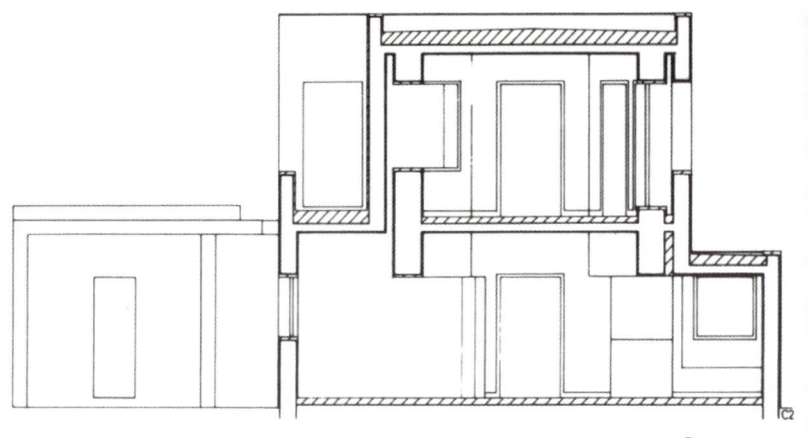

Cross section

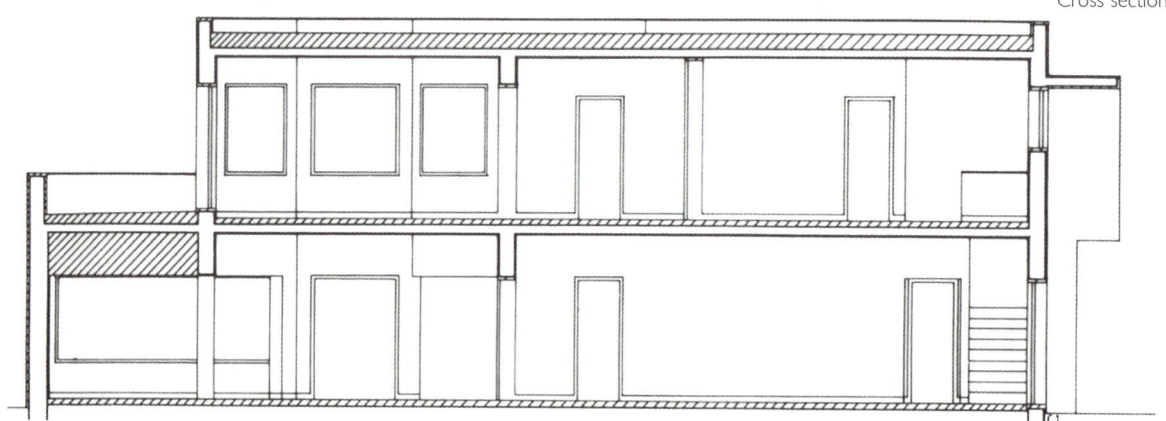

Longitudinal section

Rob Dubois & Shuichi Kobari

Sasaki-Tei

Tsukidate, Japan

Photographs: Sinichi Satou & Shuichi Kobari

In the design of this project, Sasaki House, it was essential to strike the right contrast with the large parking lot for Kurihara Auditorium, located alongside the western edge of the site, and to create a dialogue between a volume yet to be built and the bamboo grove which grows on the southern side, where the ascending slope of the site ends. On the one hand, the large parking lot would lend a certain monumental quality to its surroundings, but on the other, it was likely to bring with it a number of disadvantages: it would channel the strong wind that blows from Kurikoma Peak and leave the house exposed to the heat of the summer sun. Furthermore, it would open the house up to unwanted public views when concerts are held at the Auditorium. An extended volume was therefore planned on a north-south axis alongside the parking lot. This cuts off the strong wind, noise and the public eye and enables the creation of a calm, private space: the living room.

The western facade of the house is defined by two layers of skin; the inner one, designed in accordance with the function the space demands of it, is staggered to avoid glare from the setting sun, whereas the outer one, built in rust-proof metal mesh, is more uniform and prevents leaves and snow transported by the wind from forming drifts, as well as blocking the view from the parking lot.

The southern edge of the plot is delimited by a grove of tall bamboo, which provides a pleasant view but has the negative affect of blocking the light in the winter, when the sun is lower in the sky. To combat this, a horizontal opening was created at the top of the building. The solidity of concrete was chosen as the building material for the ground floor, to communicate the image of continuity with the ground. This contrasts with the volume of the first floor, which incorporates two diagonal cuts and is built in a lighter material, wood, to express the relationship with the bamboo and its whimsical, fan-like growth pattern.

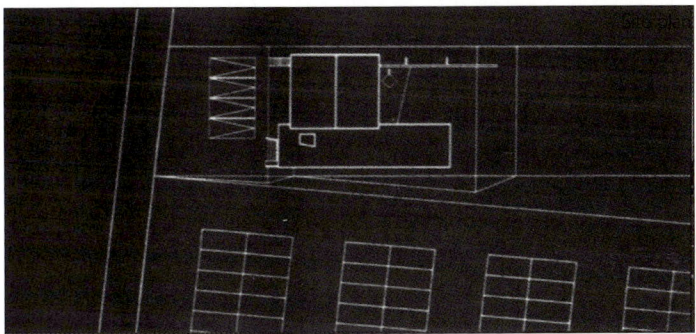

The north-south extension of the volume avoids the intrusion of views from the parking lot. The succession of photos and plans show the dialogue of the building with the surrounding artificial elements, such as the parking lot and the urban landscape dominated by an auditorium along with the natural conditions: sunlight, wind and vegetation.

"One of the most important things in the first phase of design is to seek a reciprocal relationship with the surroundings, to define the reaction that it will have with the environmental conditions around it and to reflect this conceptual interpretation in the project."

(Shuichi Kobari)

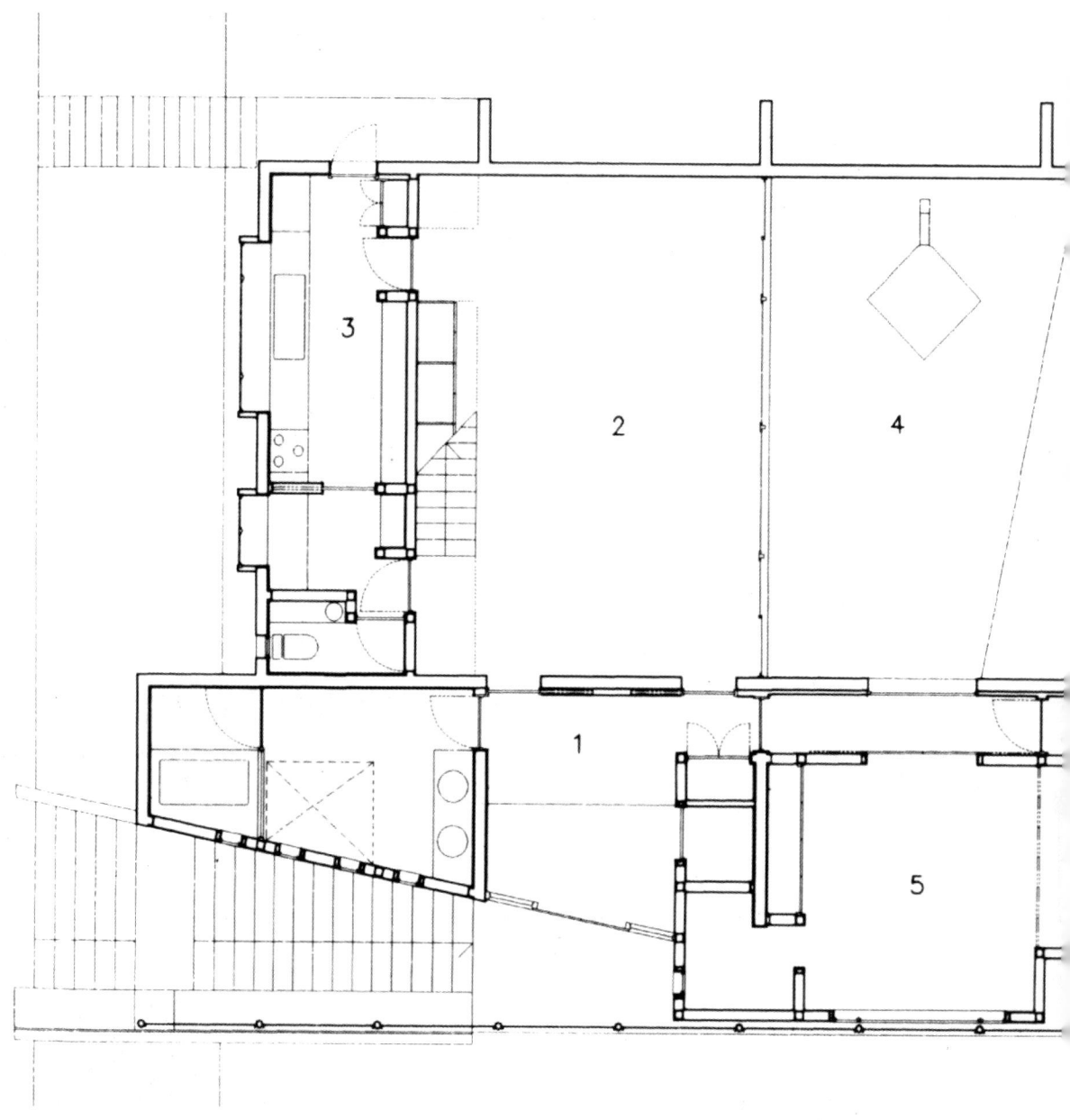

Using a clear, simple floor plan, three spaces with different characteristics were created: an open, west-facing volume, behind which sits the more private ground floor and, finally, the first floor with open views of the sky as well as of the nearby bamboo thicket.

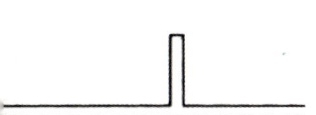

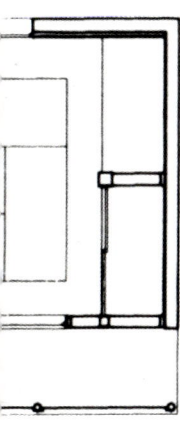

Ground floor plan

1. Entry hall
2. Living room
3. Kitchen
4. Terrace
5. Bed room
6. Japanese room

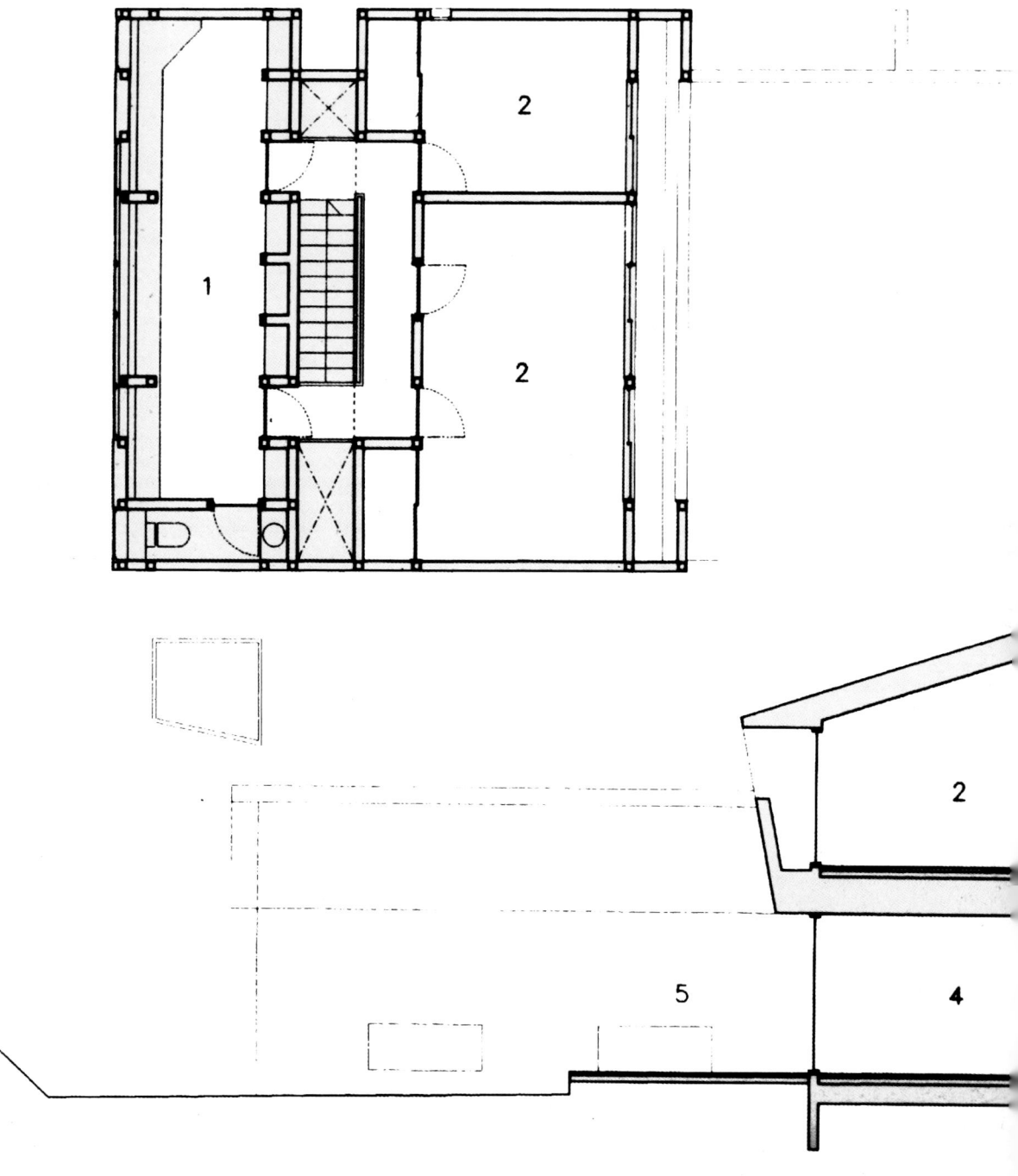

First floor plan

1. Library
2. Bedroom
3. Kitchen
4. Living room
5. Terrace

The interior space combines the Western principle of division of functions (each room having a specific use) with the subtleties of traditional Japanese practices and spaces.

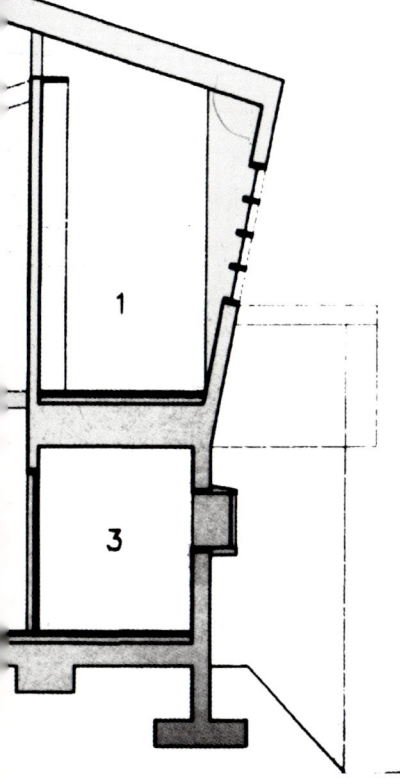

Bart Prince

Hight Residence

Mendocino, USA

Photographs: Alan Weintraub/Prince

The Hight Residence is on a beautiful two-acre site on the cliffs overlooking the Pacific Ocean near the village of Mendocino, California. It is designed to function initially as a holiday or weekend home, but will become the owner's main residence in a few years. It is sited to take advantage of the views to the south and southwest, while shielding the occupants from the near-constant winds from the north. On the ground floor, the house is divided at the entry by a breezeway, which separates the garage with guestroom above from the main living areas and other bedrooms. The cedar-shingled, glue-laminated undulating roof divides at this entry point to allow the visitor to take cover from the wind and rain and yet see right through the structure to the sea and rock islands beyond.

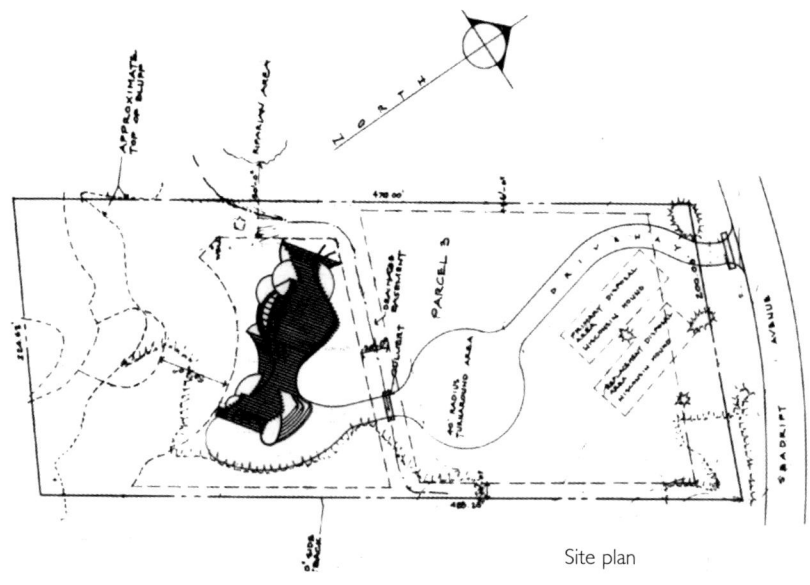

Site plan

Ground floor plan

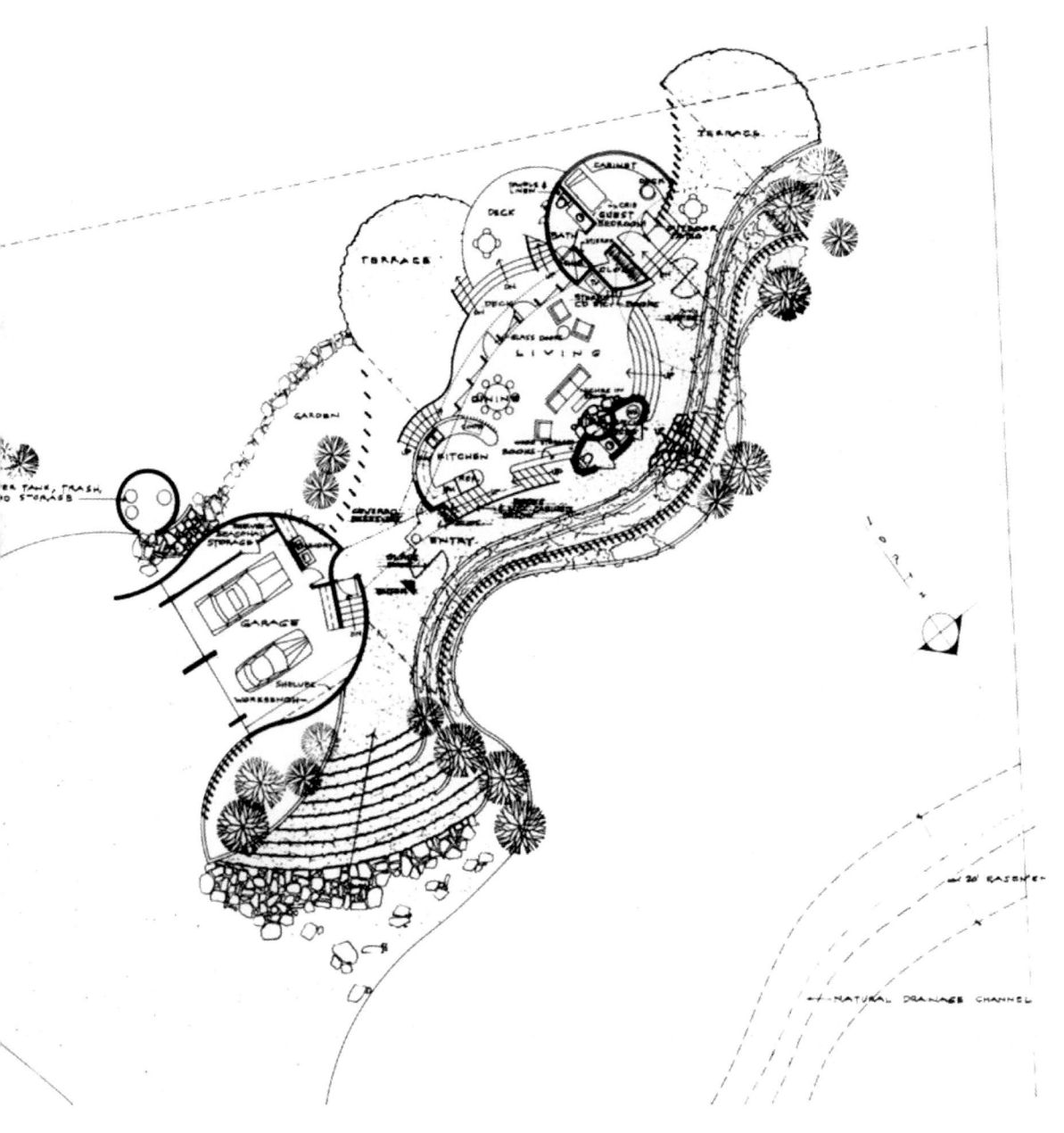

The structures are not simply frames on which the architecture rests, but rather they form an integral part of the design. The spaces are generated on the basis of the internal structure and are expressed in the external appearance. On the north side the roof reaches the ground to channel the wind over the house, whereas the south side is open, with terraces oriented toward the best views.

First floor plan

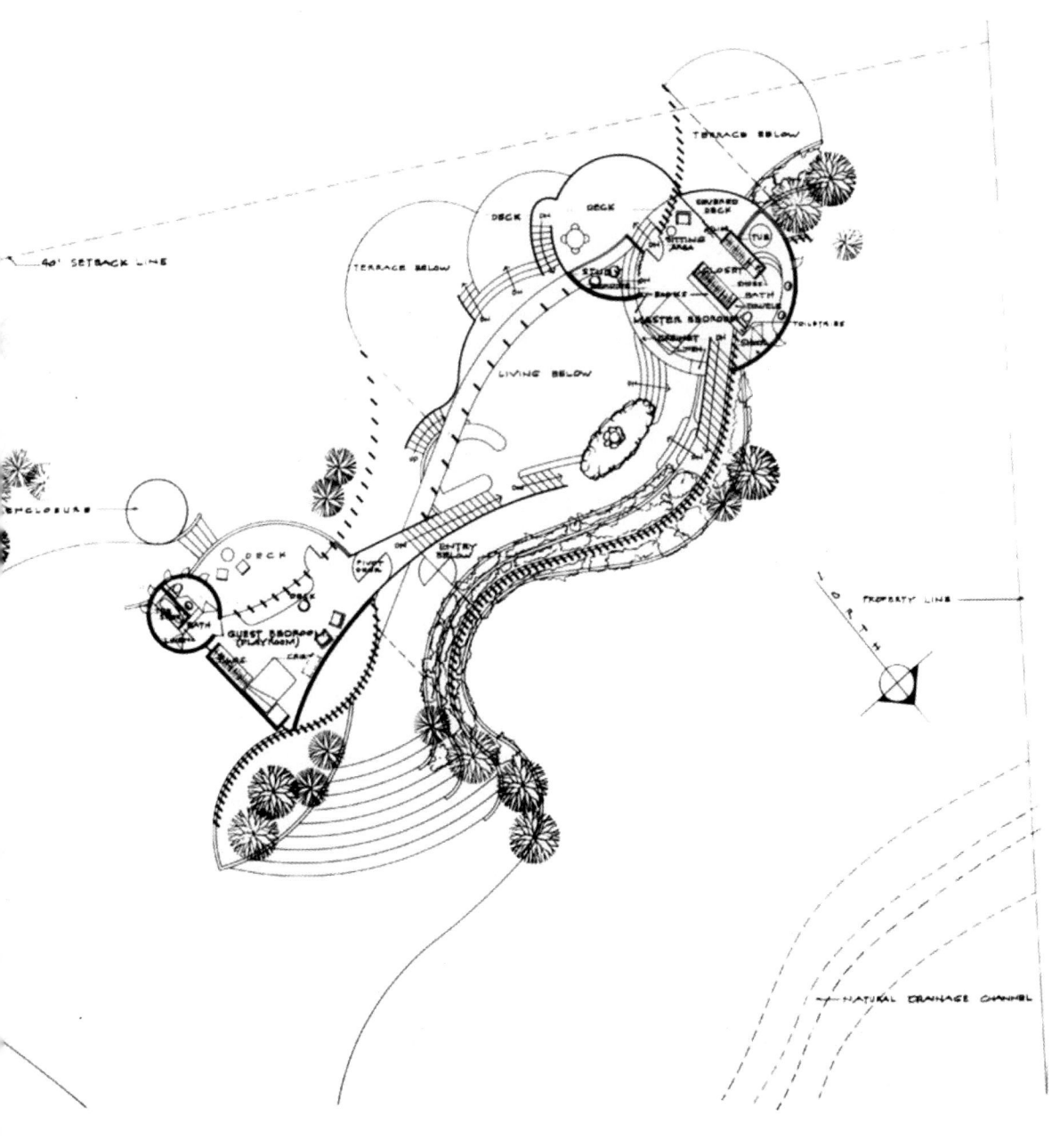

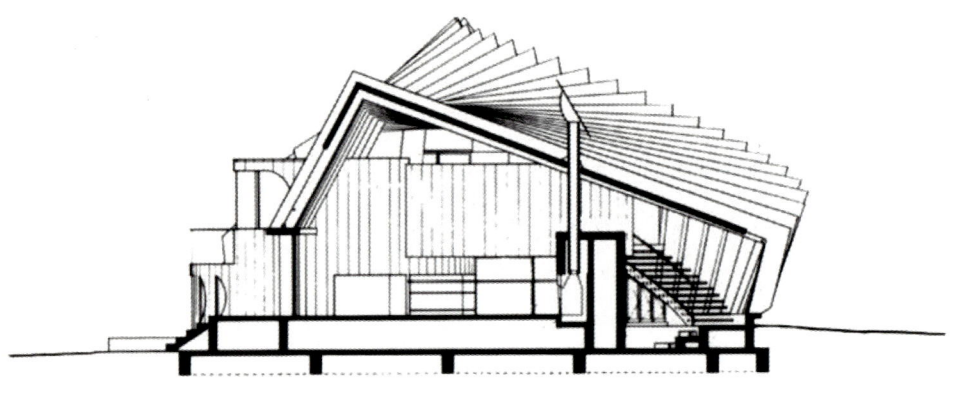

SECTION C·C   ¼"·1'·0"   SECTION

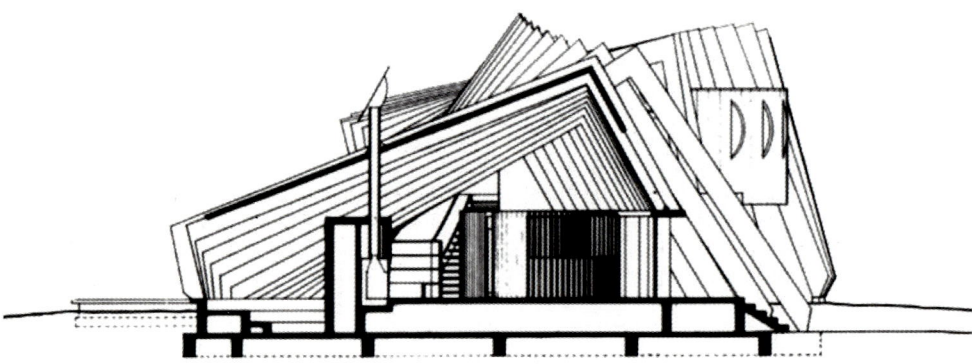

SECTION D·D   ¼"·1'·0"   SECTION

Cross sections

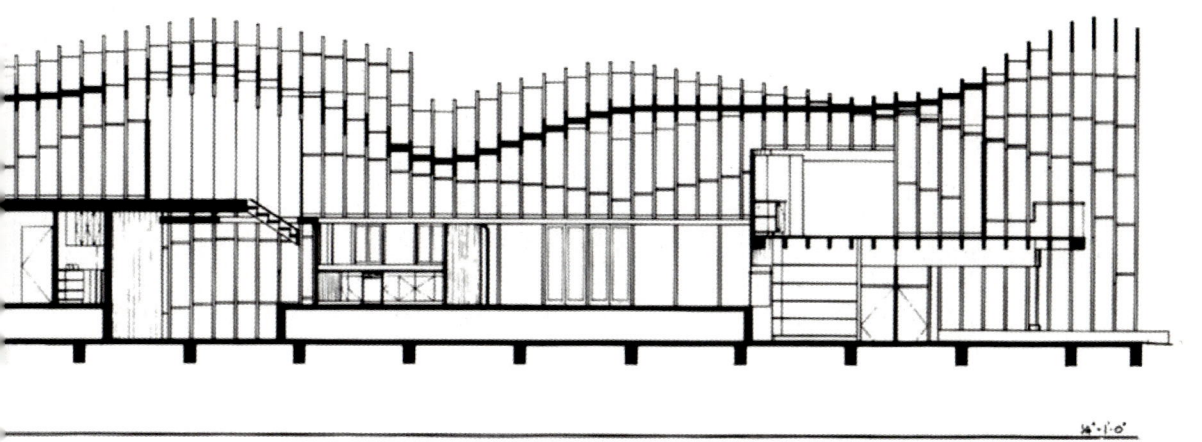

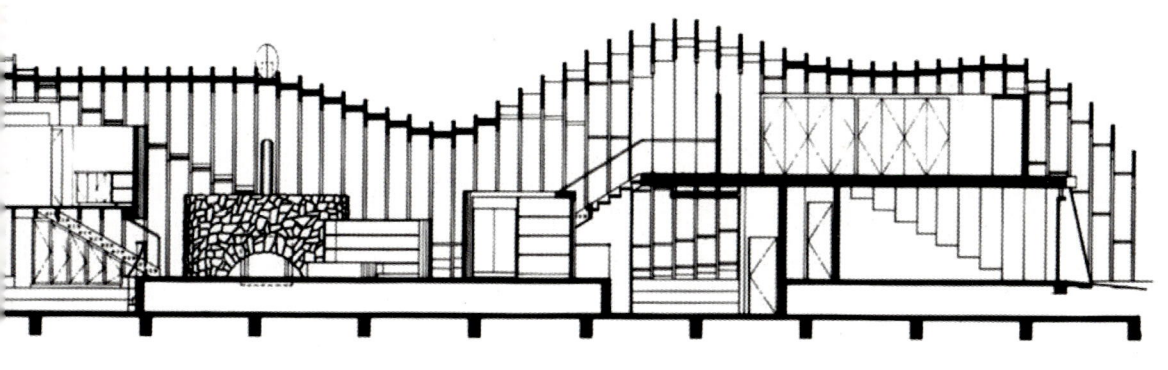

Longitudinals sections

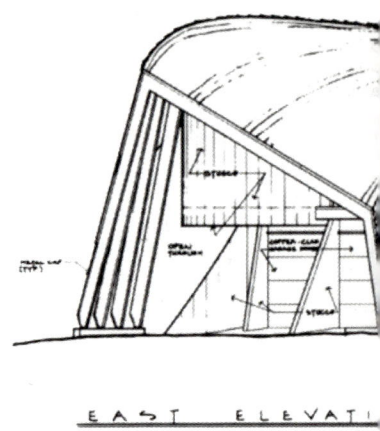

East elevation

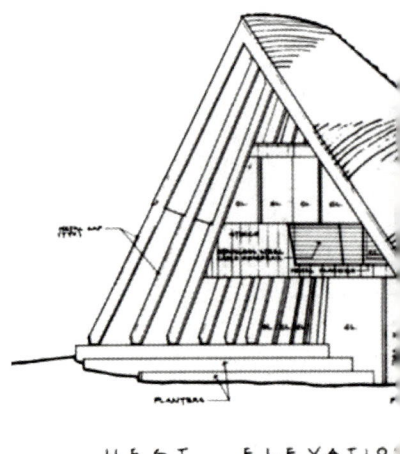

West elevation

In Bart Prince's design philosophy, influenced by that of Bruce Goff, each project corresponds to a particular situation and a particular client, and as such is a unique creative experience in which imitation has no place.

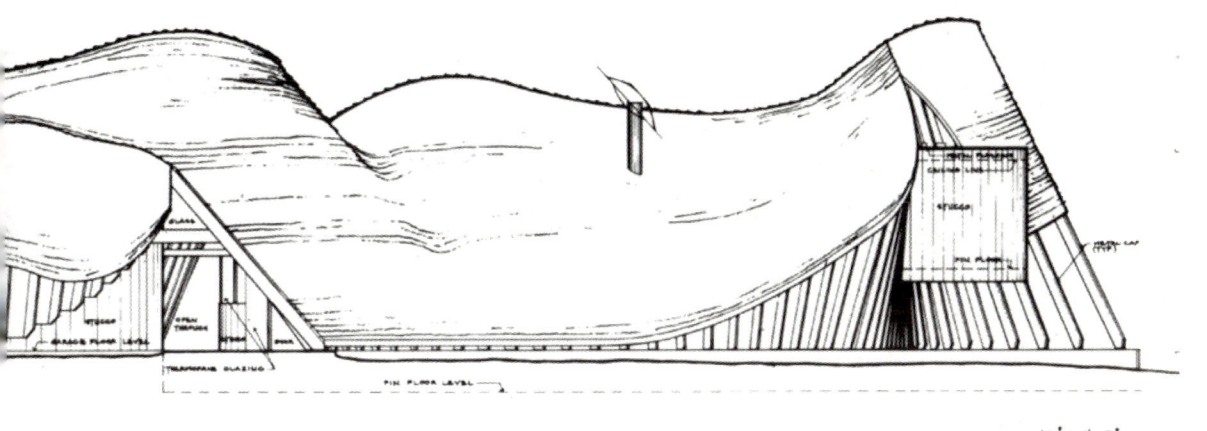

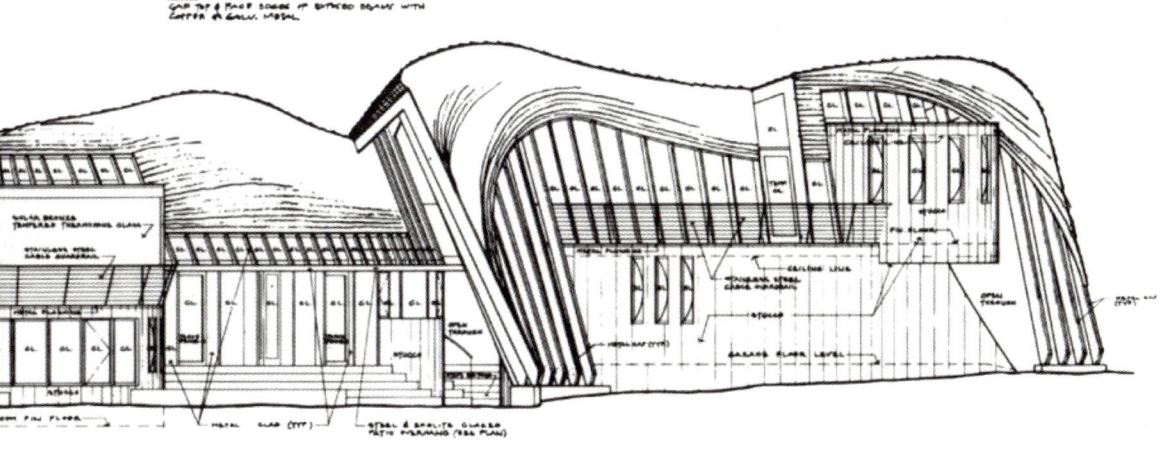

Bart Prince

Gradow Family Residence

Aspen, USA

Photographs : Robert Reck, Barbi Benton y Bart Prince

Bart Prince's project for the Gradow family in Aspen, Colorado, is on a considerably larger site (40 acres) with spectacular views in all directions.

The client wanted to see these views from every room; thus, the design climbs the hill in steps, each grouping of spaces looking out over these below. The main entry by a long stairway-gallery or by elevator, to the large living area below, bounded on one side by a curving frameless glass wall overlooking the mountains and valleys. Above this are four structures which mount the hill progressively. From the bottom up, the various levels contain: the master bedroom suite, children's bedrooms and guest quarters, the offices and staff area with a photography dark room, and finally, the gym and lap pools. The translucent sidewalls of the lap pool room slide open in good weather to completely expose the distant views across the valley.

Site plan

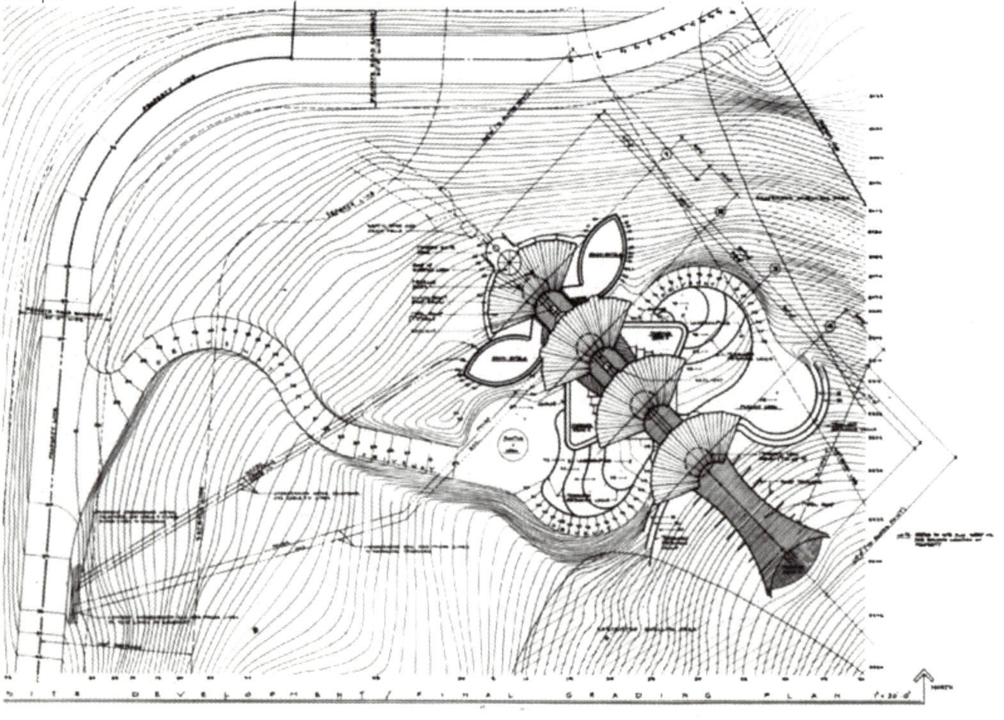

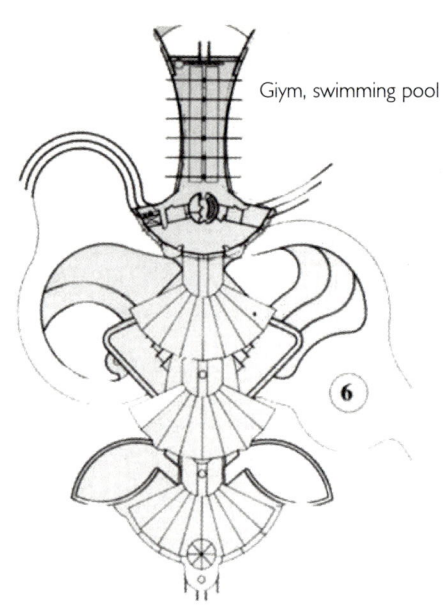
Giym, swimming pool

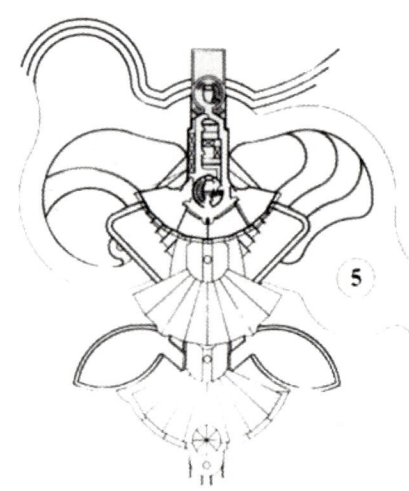
Offices, dark room

Guest bedroom, children's bedroom

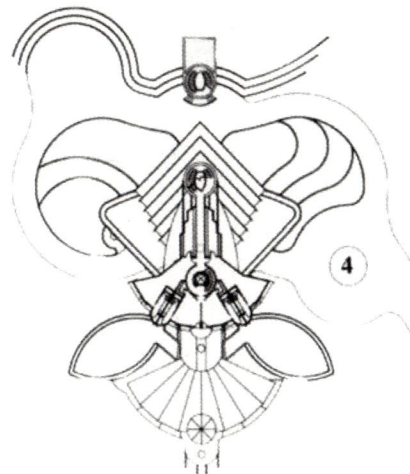

Master bedroom

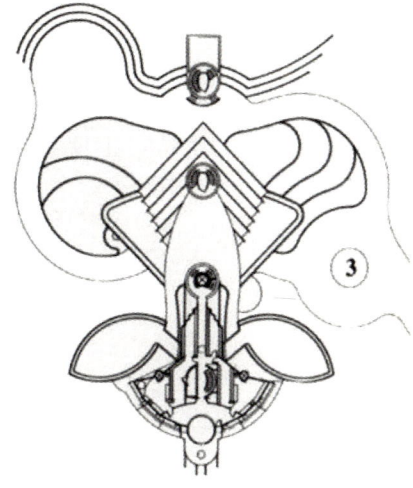

Succession of plans from the topmost level to the bottommost
6. Living room, lounge, kit
5. Dining room, entrance, terra
4. Master bedroom
3. Guest bedroom & children's bedroom
2. Offices, dark room
1. Gym, swimming

Dining room, entrance, terraces

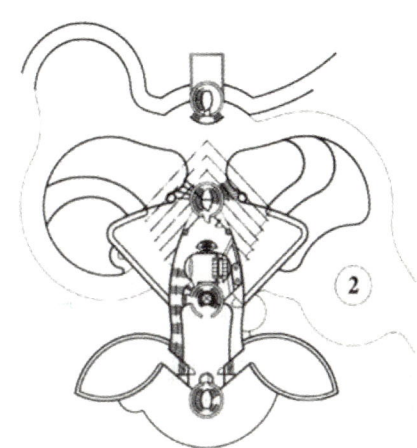

Living room, disco, kitchen

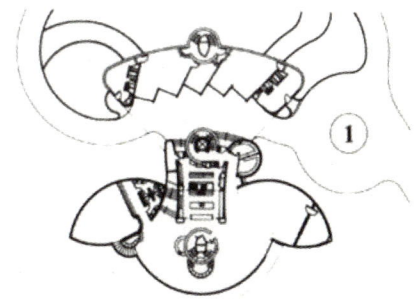

Although its form adapts to the terrain, the house is integrated into the landscape by contraposition, particularly in good weather, when the reflection of the extensive surfaces of glass and copper cuts a powerful silhouette.

The house cascades down the mountainside in a series of fan-shaped volumes affording panoramic views.

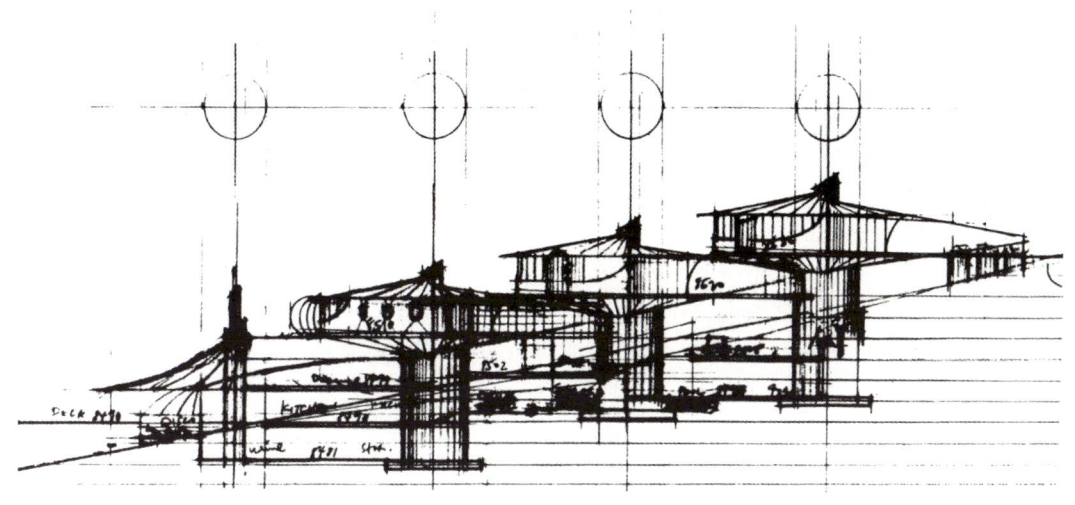

The combination of materials is quite unusual. The exterior finish of these "pod" structures is copper and glass. The structural system is steel frame with wood frame infill supported on reinforced concrete and masonry service cores, which contain the stairs, elevator, and mechanical and electrical equipment.

Harry Seidler & Associati

Farrell House

Sydney, Australia

Photographs: Eric Sierins

This house for a family with two teenage boys is built on a suburban site with an oblique view toward Sydney Harbor.

The typologically very original parti shows a construction at the same time turned in on itself around the spiral staircase and strongly connected to the exterior by the striking projection of the curved balcony of prestressed concrete, glass and metal.

The house is curved in the direction of the view, the living room and master bedroom opening over it. The opposing view to the rear is over the garden, dominated by a huge eucalyptus. The ground slopes up from the street, locating the main floor on a level with the garden, over which the family room opens to reveal the swimming pool, built against the back boundary.

The focal point of the house is the spiral staircase, with its large overhead skylight, around which the corridorless plan revolves. In order to maintain a visually transparent environment, the living room, family room, dining room and study and guestroom are separated by glass walls and doors.

The upper floor contains four bedrooms, each with private bathroom, while the ground floor houses the entrance hall, double garage and playroom.

The edges of the concrete floors are expressed on the exterior, projecting down over ribbon windows. The walls are of concrete blocks specially formulated to expose selected aggregate on their polished exterior.

All outdoor glass is installed without any framing, even the curved sliding doors being of toughened glass. Protection from the sun is provided by vertical aluminum blades bracketed to the structural supports.

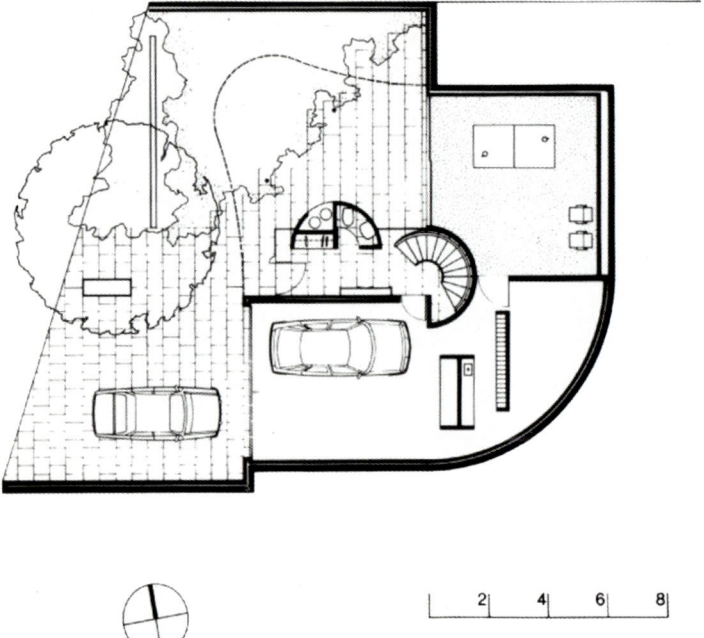

Ground floor plan

First floor plan

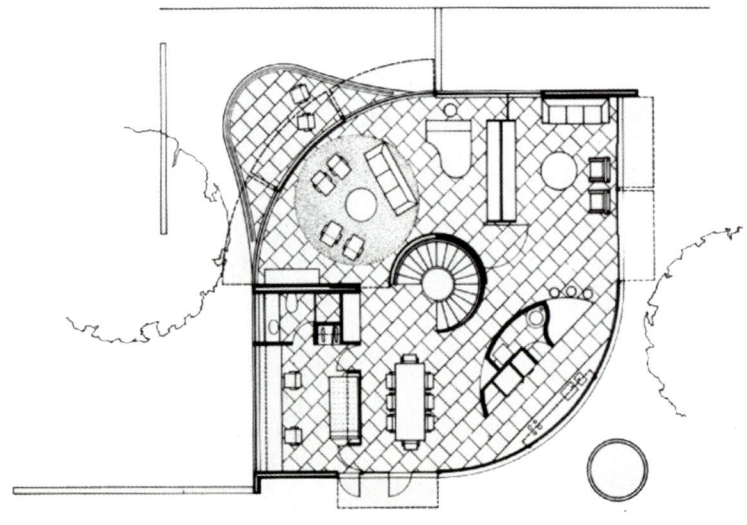

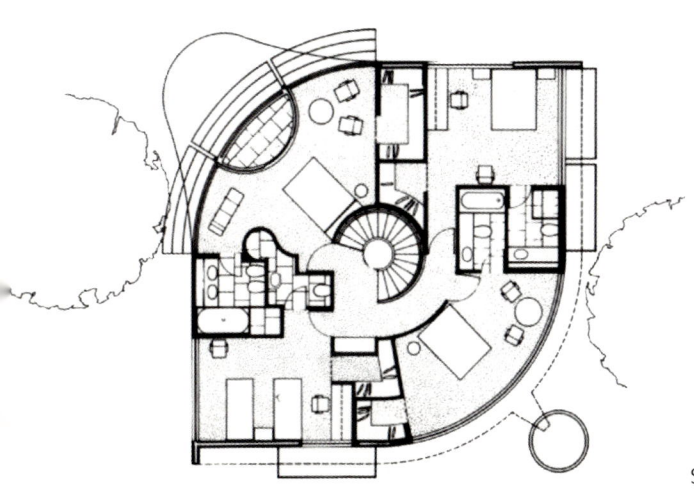

Second floor plan

The Farrell House possesses great sculptural qualities. The curved lines of the aluminum sun screens contrast with the sobriety of the concrete walls.

The finish of the specially formulated concrete blocks, polished to show the gravel and other materials of which it is comprised, contrasts with the clean cut of the aluminum and glass.

The two opposing quadrants cut off the corners of the square plan of the house. The most handsome effect is achieved in the balance between the flat surface of the facade and its dominating curve.

The glass and concrete of the balcony creates a highly theatrical effect at night.

Shin Takamatsu & Associati

Iwai House

Minami-ku, Japan

Photographs: Nacása & Partners

Alone in open fields on the edge of town, in an almost defenseless site beyond an industrial belt, stands this two-story private house, built in reinforced concrete and partly steel frame. On both interior and exterior, the architects have brought to bear all the expressive potential of concrete.

The most noticeable feature of the exterior is the curved wall to the left of the entrance on the main facade. Traditionally in architecture, the wall divides inside and out, yet here the curve gradually draws visitors inside and deepens the ambiguity of the relationship between the two. At first glance this convex wall seems rather aggressive, but within the residence its concavity becomes intimate.

The curved wall also forms the outer edge of a secluded courtyard, and incorporates a raised walkway and a terrace from which one can contemplate the scenery. The courtyard and the large windows overlooking it are protected by a brise-soleil.

The glazed entrance hall leads into a sinuous corridor in which the untreated structural concrete creates a fine visual balance with the wooden flooring. Concrete is left unadorned throughout much of the house, for example in the columns, and complements the plastered surfaces, largely in white with patches of primary colors.

Although the house is thoroughly modern, the interior owes a great deal of its delicacy to traditional Japanese aesthetics. The atrium leading to the terrace is a good example of the common ground that exists between the two approaches.

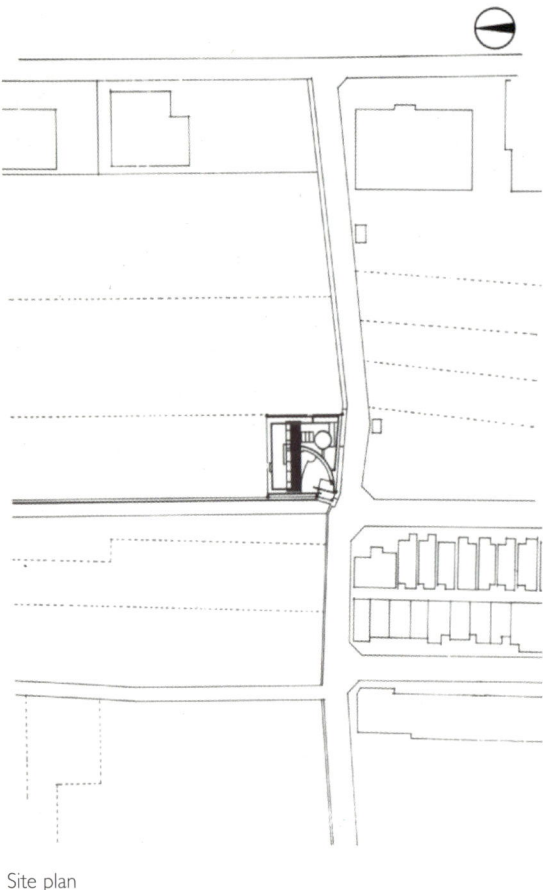

Site plan

The wide curve not only gives a feeling of protection but also allows the enjoyment of a space at once open, intimate and cool on the ground floor. On the upper level, the elevated walkway and terrace bring sun and civilization closer.

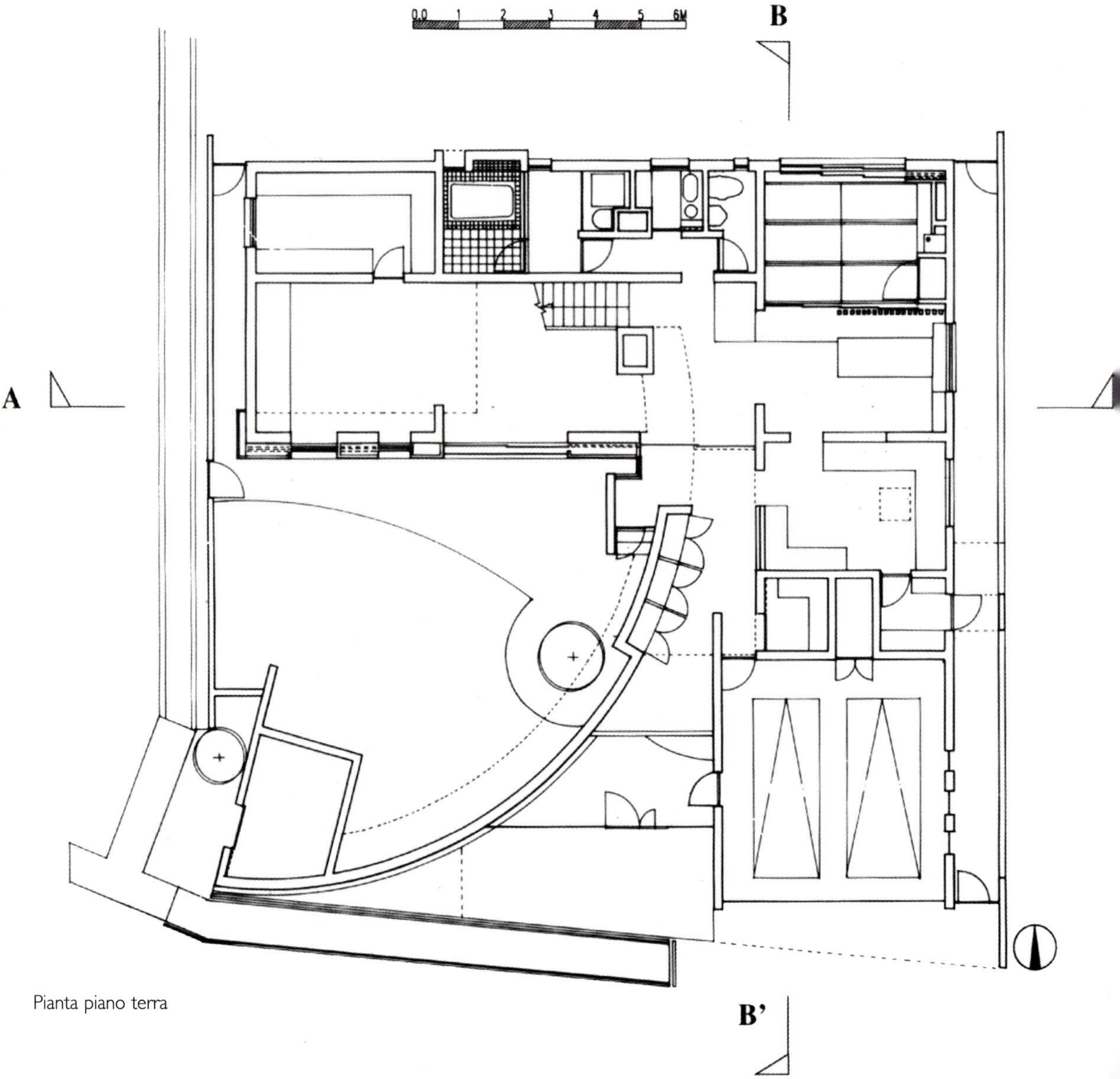

Pianta piano terra

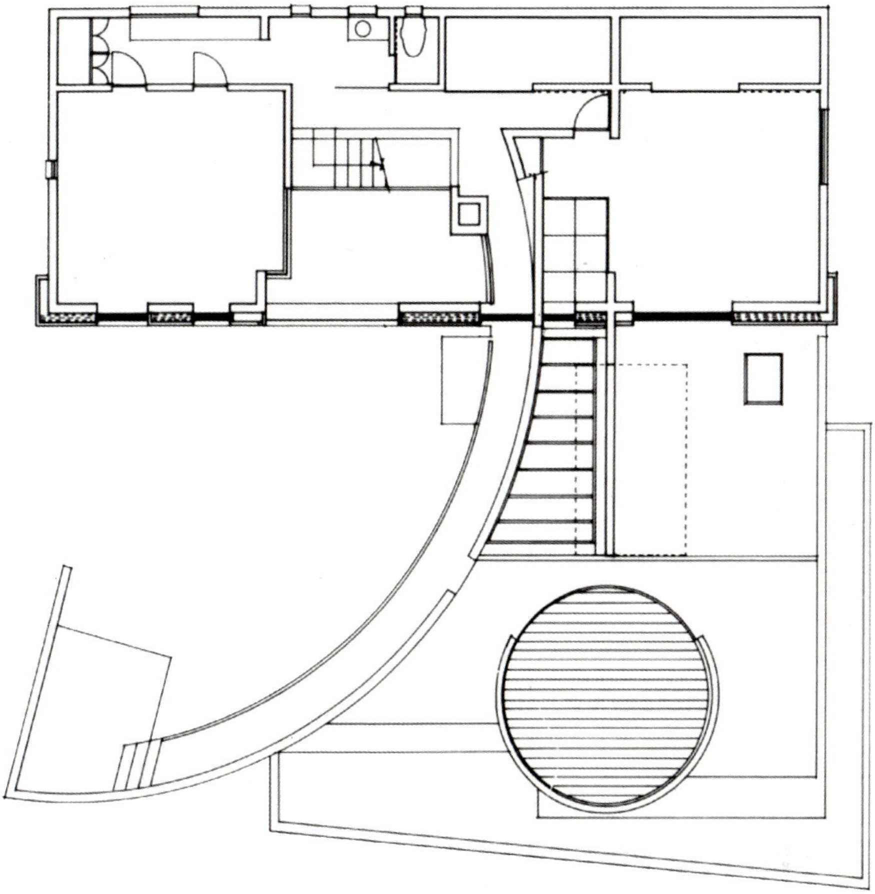

First floor plan

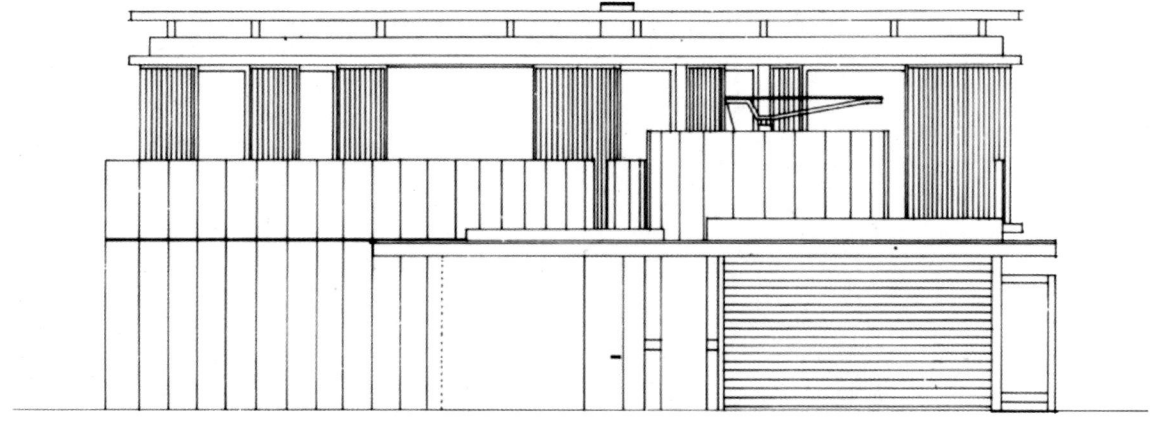

South elevation

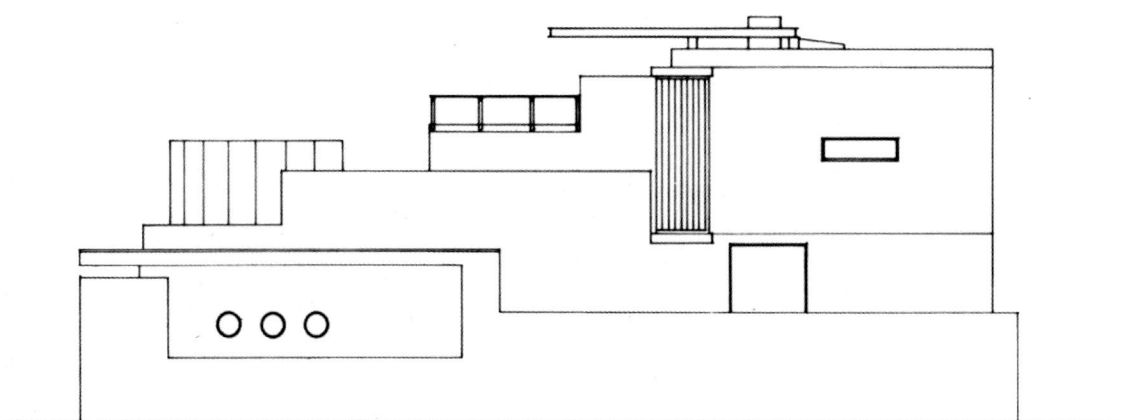

East elevation

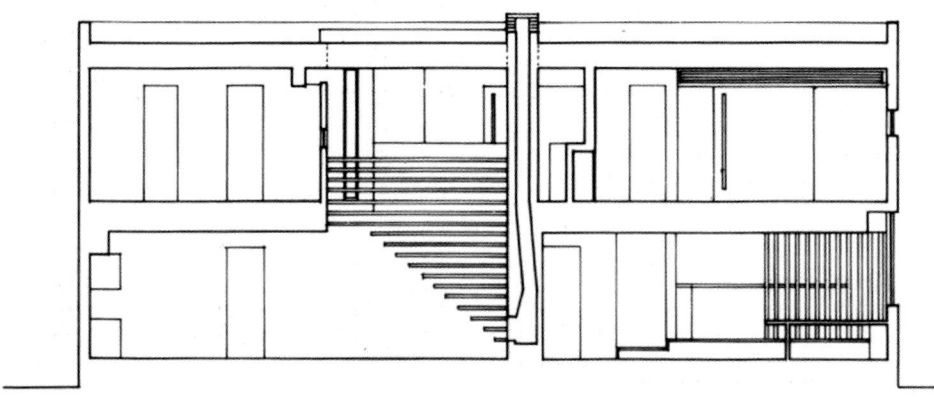

Section AA'

The interior design combines industrial production and traditional detail, rough material and finishes in primary colors.

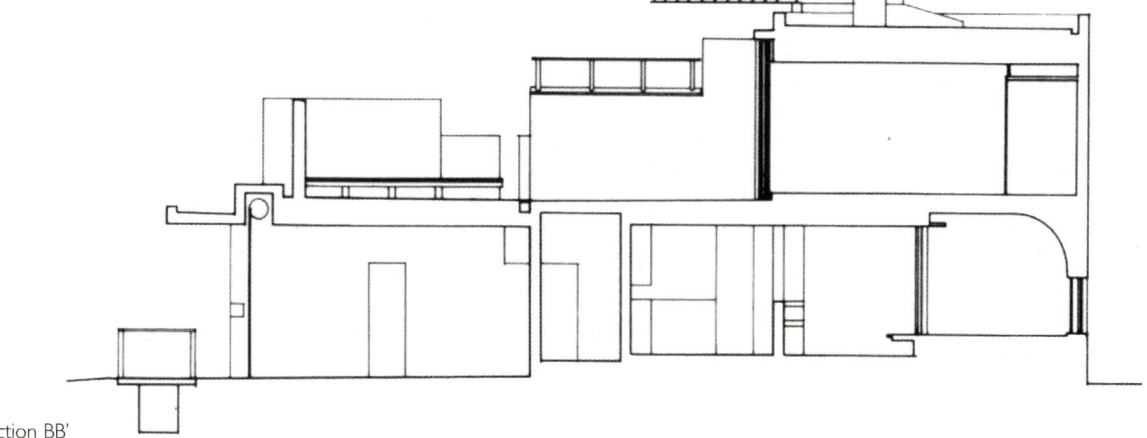

Section BB'

The architect has recreated a typically Oriental atmosphere of serenity in some of the rooms to take refuge from the chaos of Kyoto's outskirts.

"The wall gradually draws visitors inside, into its unnatural nature, as if entering the stomach of Moby Dick". (Shin Takamatsu)

Tadao Ando

Lee House

Tokyo, Japan

Photograps: Mitsuo Matsuoka

This private house is situated on a hill in suburbs not far from the Tokyo metropolitan center, Funabashi, and occupies a site area of 5210 ft2. The location of the site at an intersection and its comfortable size (in comparison with more normal dimensions in Japanese houses) have allowed the creation of numerous additional spaces to the house: courtyards, gardens and terraces.

Small garden courtyards of varying character are stacked on different levels within the house in order to grant each one a distinct realm and infuse the house with greater variety.

Overall, the house has a three-level rectangular core with a 16'4" x 68'9" floor plan. An internal atrium is positioned in the mid-section of this rectangular structure, with rooms positioned at either end. The rooms face each other across the atrium at staggered half-floor intervals, and are connected by ramps running parallel to the court.

The ground floor houses the living room and dining room where the family gathers, while individual bedrooms are arranged on the upper floors. The gentle, green slope of the garden draws close where it is viewed from the dining room. This garden invites nature into the lives of the residents, while maintaining the house's privacy by obstructing visibility from the exterior. The different garden courtyards ensure a dwelling space that offers its occupants continual rediscovery, within daily life, of their relationship with the city and nature.

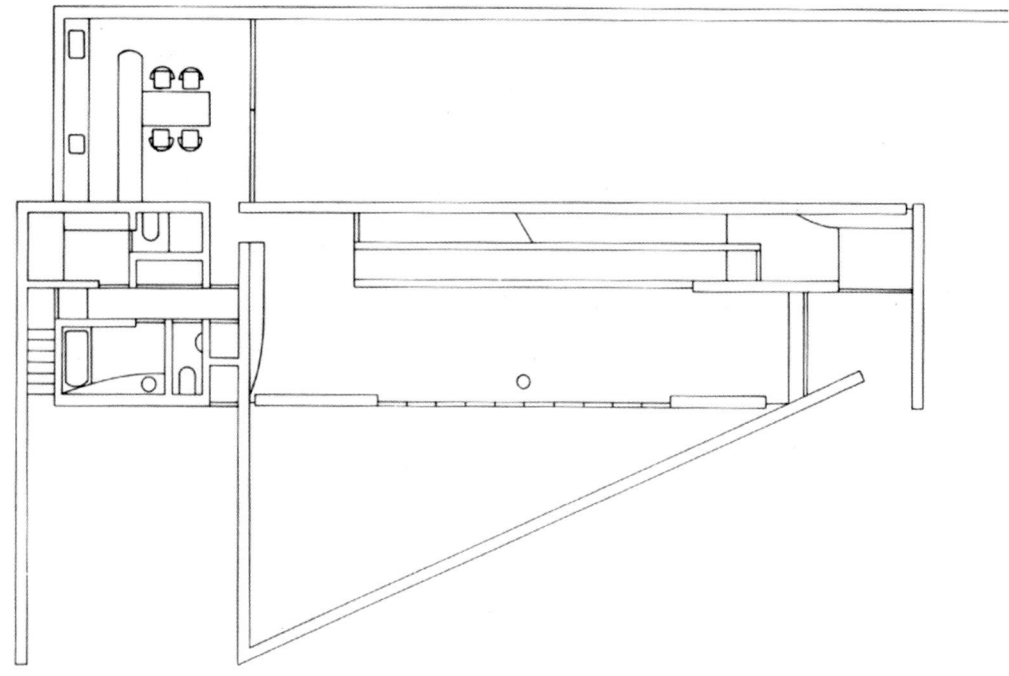

Basement floor plan

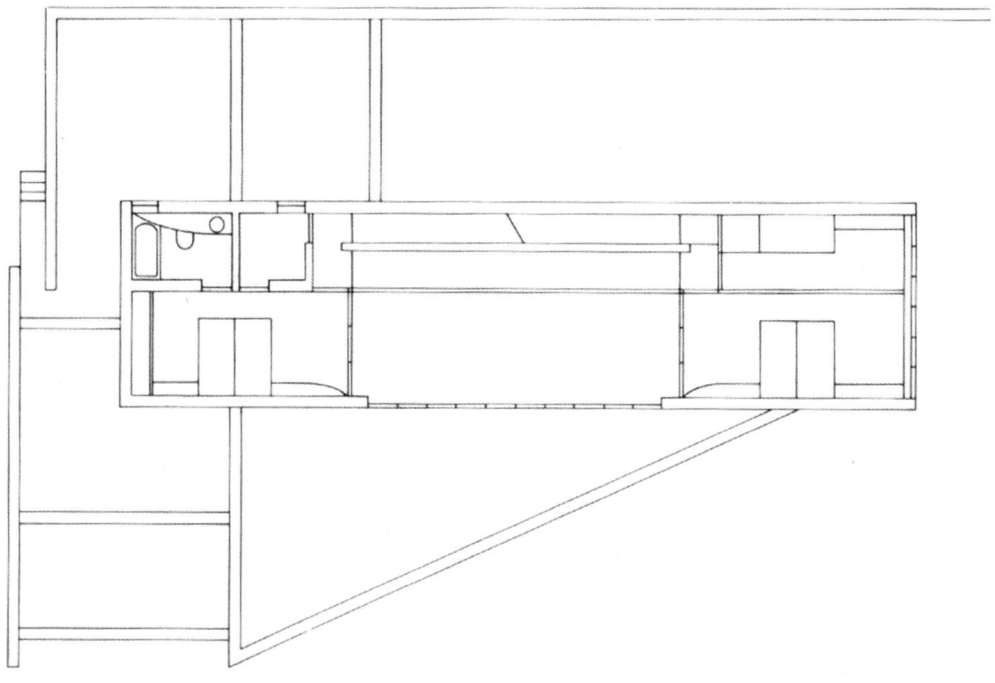

Ground floor plan

First floor plan

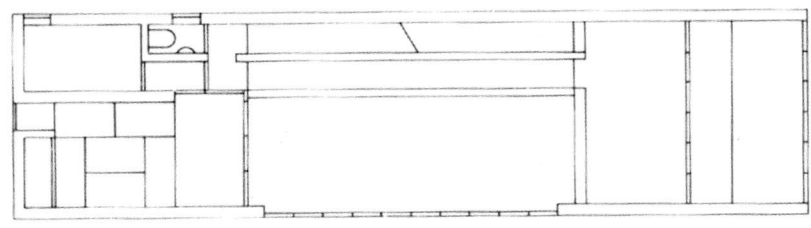

Site plan

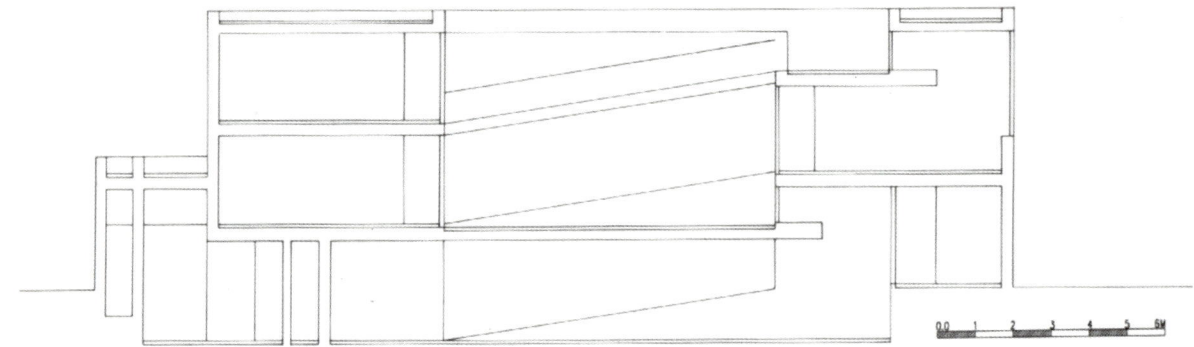

Section

The bedrooms, at staggered half-floor intervals, are connected by a ramp running parallel to the courtyard.

Stepped levels, courtyards and terraces add complexity to the project,
which is nevertheless regulated by a coherent system.

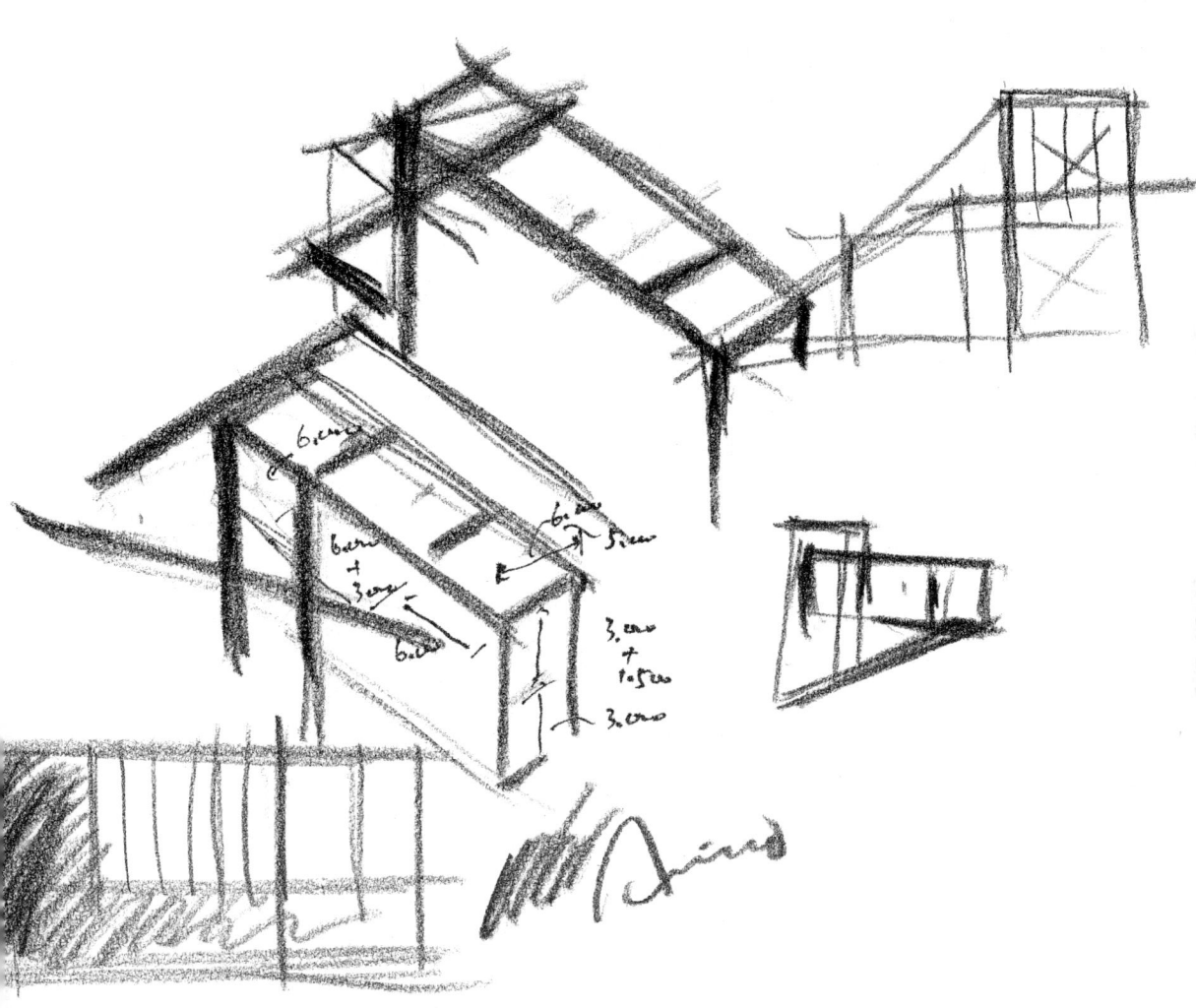

A dramatic contrast is struck between high concrete walls, the intensity of the light provided by large openings and the subtle yet notable presence of nature.
Tadao Ando skilfully combines the complexity of the spaces with the simplicity of the house's rectangular base.

Eduardo Souto de Moura

Baião House

Baião, Portugal

Photographs: Luis Ferreira Alves

For the Baião House the request of the client was to build a small residence for the weekends by restoring the old ruins of a previous building. The basic line of the project was to highlight and consolidate the remains of the old building, maintaining them as a walled garden, and to build the house completely separate.

The work began with the demolition of the supporting main wall and with the excavation for the preparation of the plot to situate the house. The house itself is a block of cement sunken into the land but open towards the River Douro. The program required a "Portuguese house", respecting the beauty of the landscape. In this case, the integration was achieved by the fact that the dwelling is very concealed; indeed, it almost appears to be buried in the surrounding terrain.

Despite the limited budget, it was possible to use materials from all over Europe: French aluminum profiles, Swiss building materials, Belgian guttering, Spanish sanitary appliances and Italian marbles and lamps, all without forgetting local materials: some pieces from the demolitions in Barredo, rubblework from Leira and elements of woodwork from Paredes. A combination and union of elements from all over the EU come together in this small holiday residence.

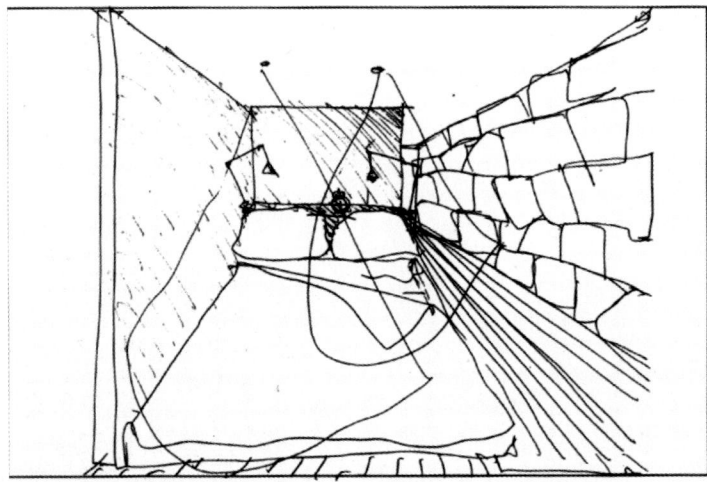

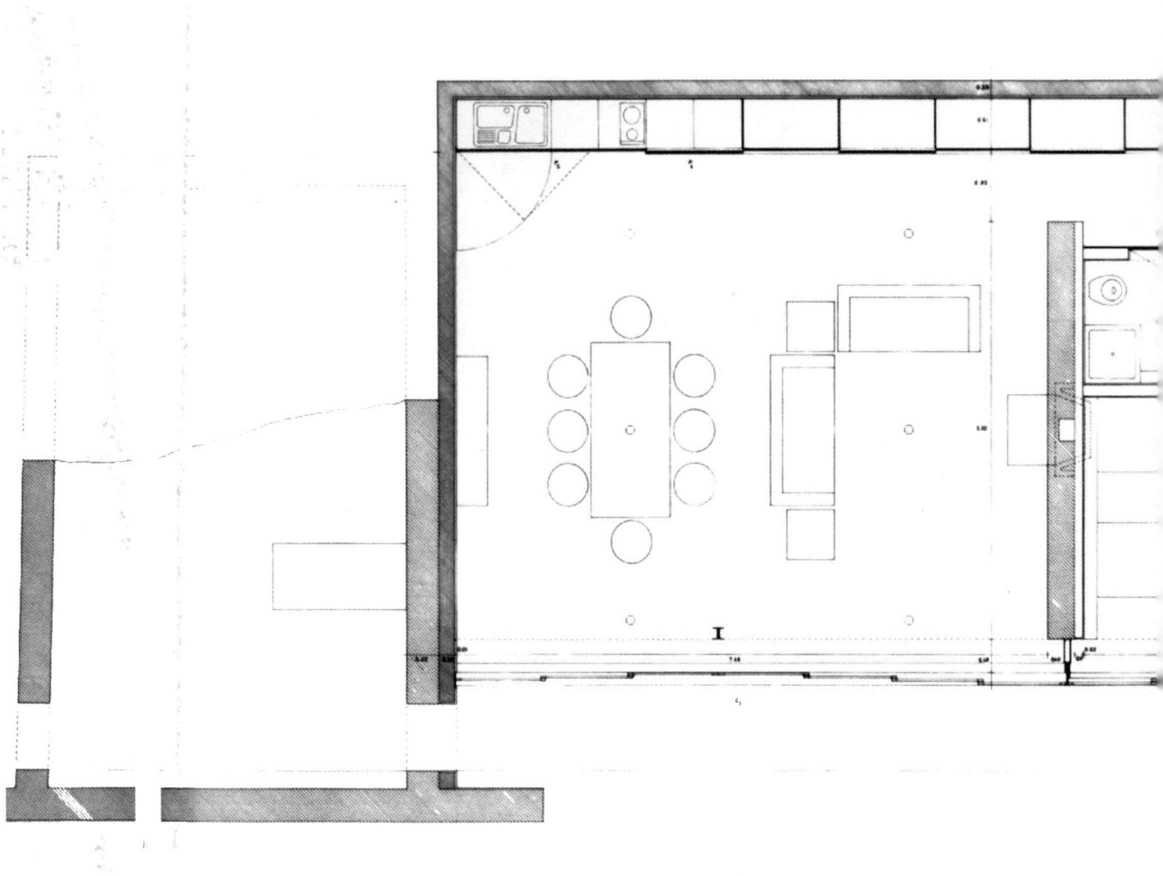

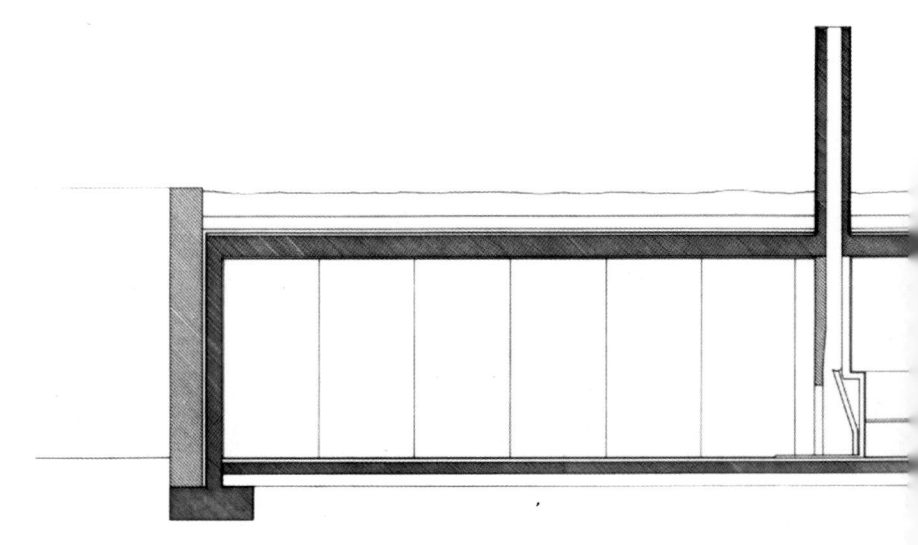

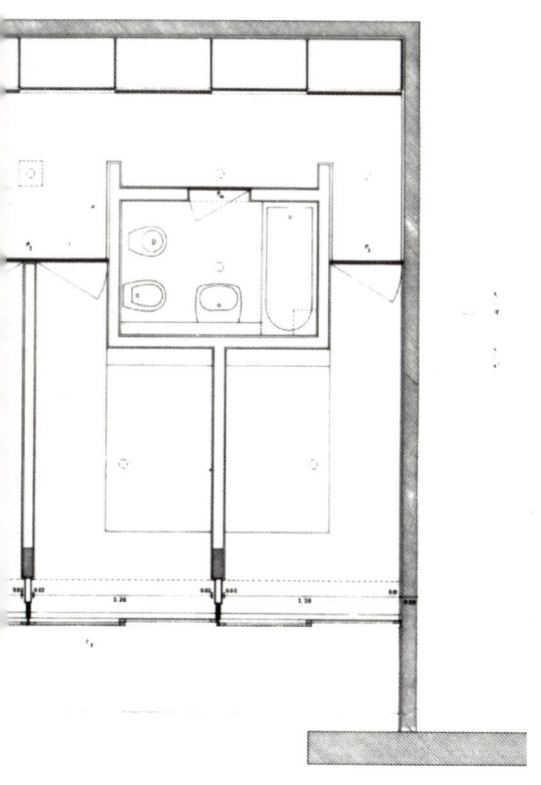

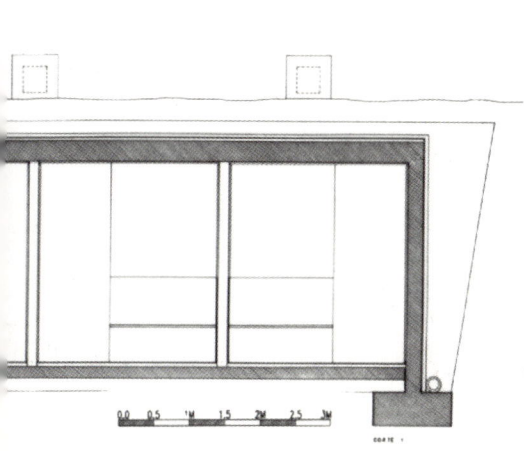

97

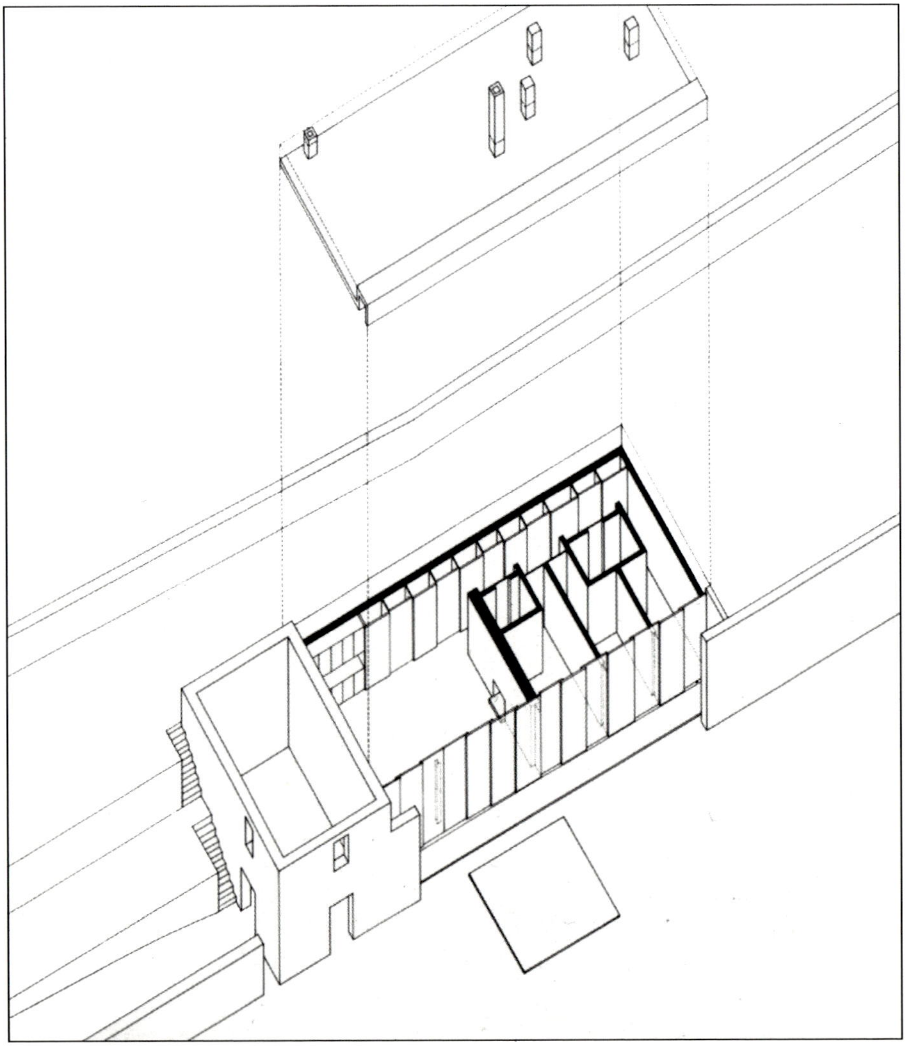

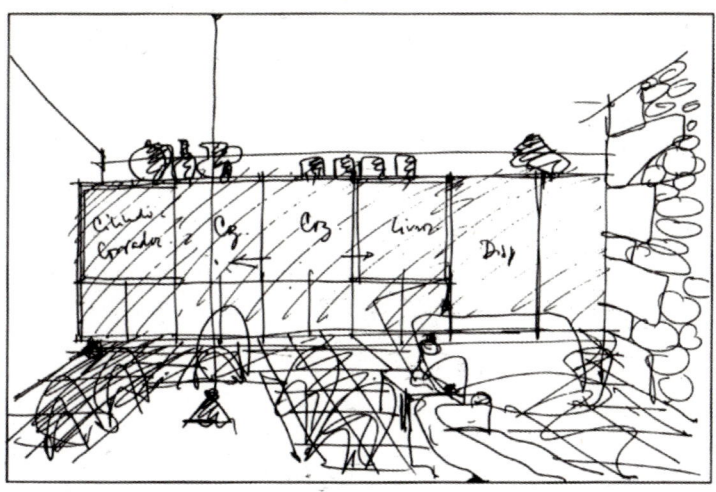

Construction detail

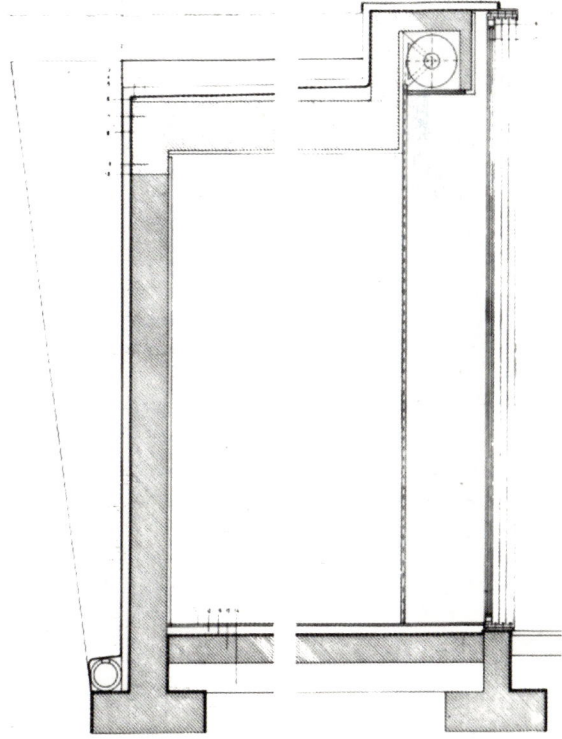

A stone wall belonging to the old ruins separates the area of the living-dining room and kitchen from the bedrooms and toilets. These two environments are communicated longitudinally by a rear corridor, with cupboards with sliding wooden doors, and opens toward the garden through sliding glass doors.

Eduardo Souto de Moura

Bom Jesus House

Braga, Portugal

Photographs: Luis Ferreira Alves

Bom Jesus was shaped by a single design, in which two different levels are combined, each with different construction techniques. Indeed, the two houses were conceived and built as a single one.

The first level, for the children, consists of an opus incertum, a stone cube with doors and windows. The second level, that of the parents, is a concrete cube with a large glazed balcony.

The meticulous attention that Souto de Moura pays not only to architectural space and form, but also to the effects produced by the materials both in the interior and the exterior can be clearly appreciated in these two projects.

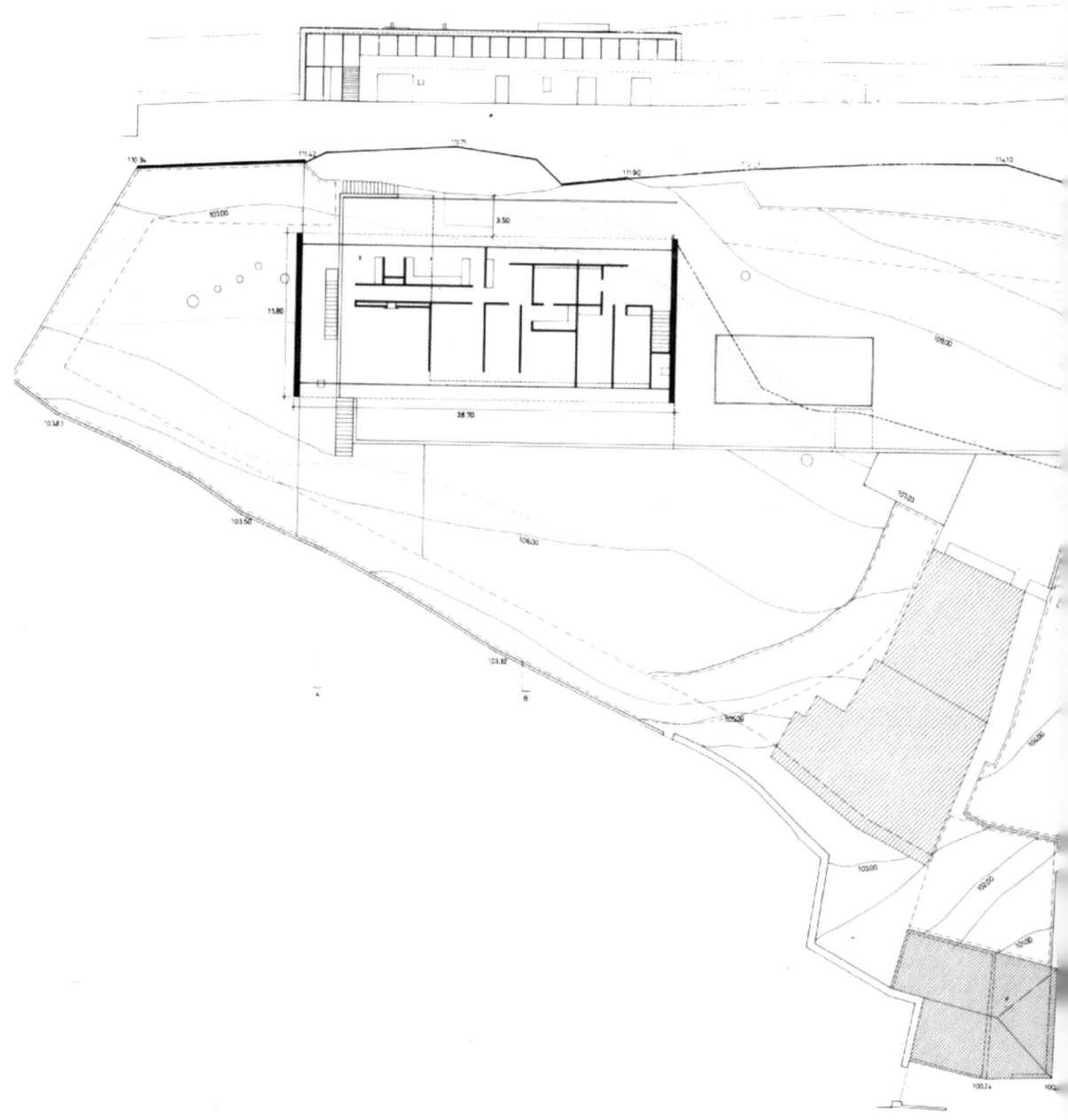

Site plan

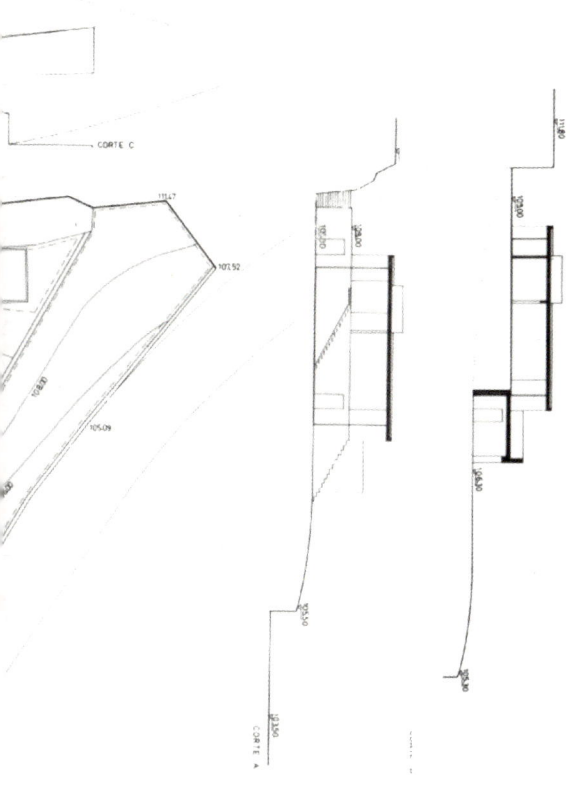

Ground floor plan

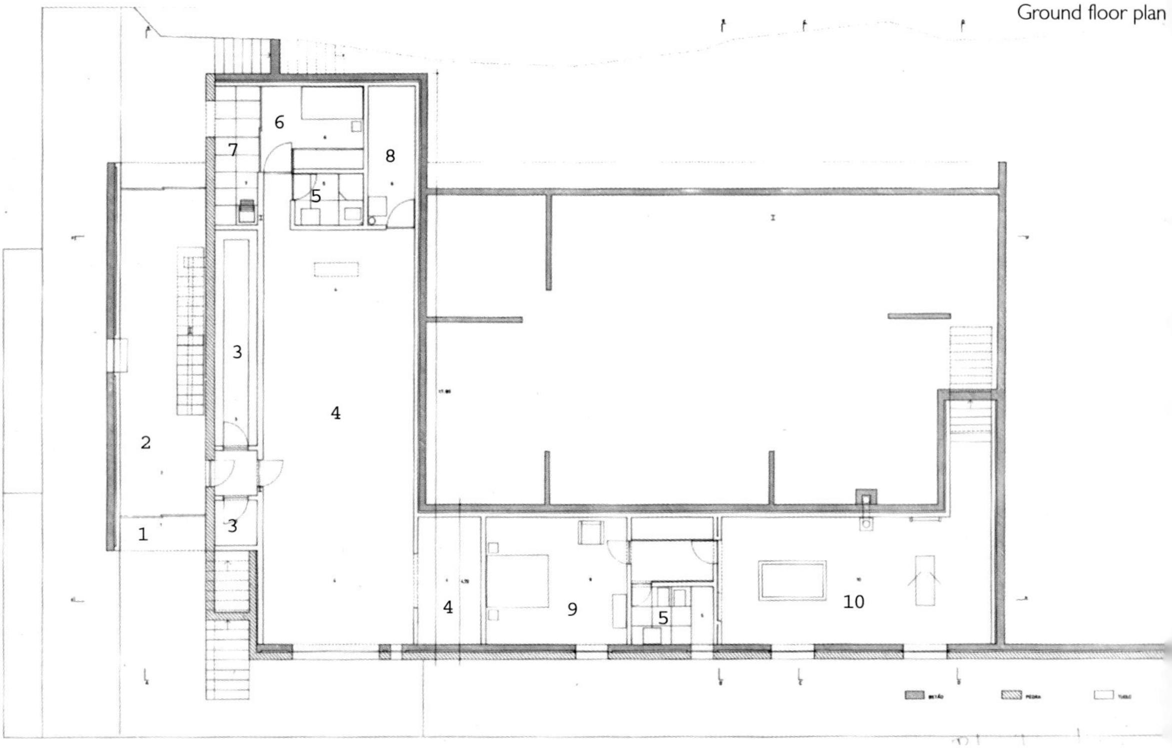

First floor plan

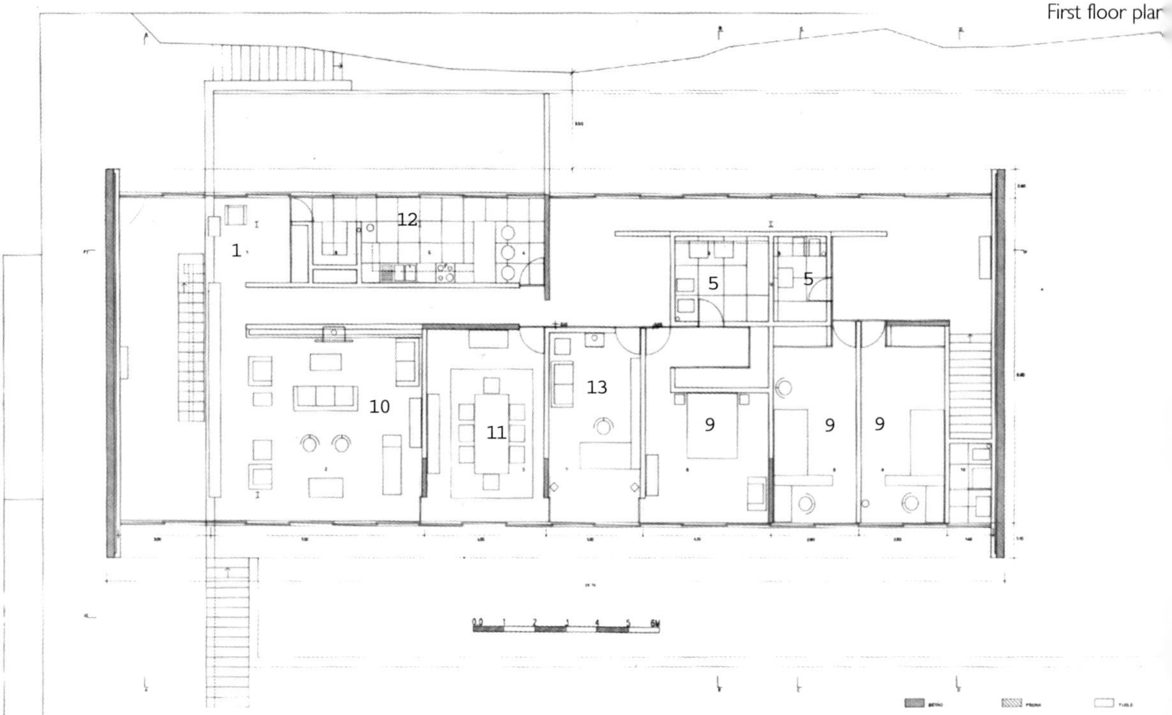

1. Access
2. Hall
3. Storage
4. Garage
5. WC
6. Staff
7. Wash room

8. Machine room
9. Bedroom
10. Living room
11. Dining room
12. Kitchen
13. Study

On the ground floor (the children's area) the use of traditional materials is predominant: stone, wood and clay tiles, which have been skilfully combined with a glass wall with aluminum profiles. The building details of this floor transmit the sensations of the different finishes: smooth, polished, rough, fragile, solid, natural, and artificial.

Daniele Marques & Bruno Zurkirchen

Kraan Lang House

Emmenbrücke, Switzerland

Photographs: Daniel Mayer

The plot for which the single-family dwelling was to be designed is located in an area with a heterogeneous planning situation, a zone of agglomeration in which the urban fabric gives way to the countryside. Buildings of varying uses populate the vicinity: farm buildings, cubic zigzag apartment blocks built in the sixties, and in a concrete single-family dwelling.

The aim of the architectural design was to respond to the planning regulations by means of two floors consisting of an ephemeral container in opposition to the more solid neighboring constructions. Both floors are south facing.

The living area opens onto a covered veranda, the top of which is slightly lower than the top of the sliding windows, thus allowing a strip of natural light to enter the living space. The north side is closed in order to shut off unwanted views of the nearby railway line.

The position of the container, in exact relation to the neighboring concrete single-family dwelling, is intended to define an exterior space belonging to both houses. The single-family dwelling is prefabricated, the constructional system being based on large panels for light constructions and pillars resting on a pedestal in the basement. It is covered with untreated trapezoidal aluminum sheet. This aluminum cladding was used for all the exterior surfaces, including the roof. The remaining wooden constructional elements were left untreated, except for a wax coating.

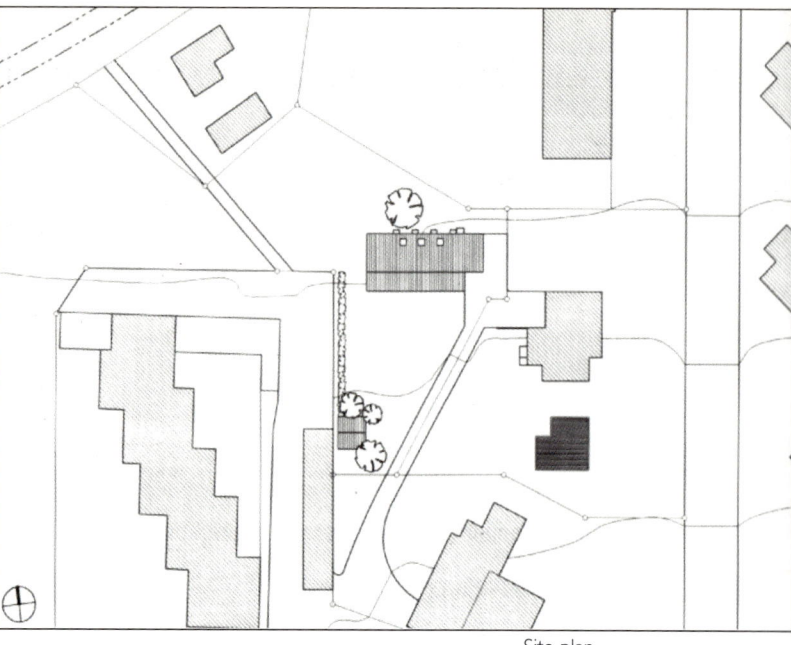

Site plan

A study of the environment of the project enables us to define the spatial logic of the building. The model shows the desire of the architects to distinguish them from the progressive development of this formerly rural area, which is now a total planning chaos. The site plan shows how the articulation with the neighboring concrete house manages to create a more formalized exterior space.

Ground floor plan

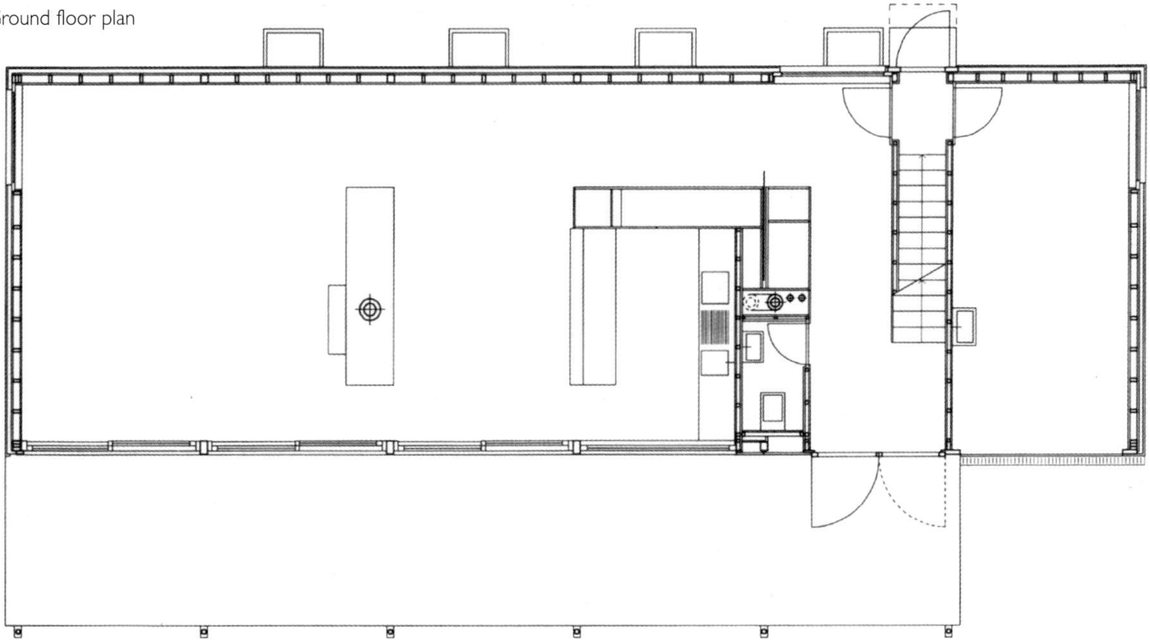

The large aluminum panels that recall industrial containers create an unexpected and subversive effect in the context and give an air of nobility to the house despite their low cost and ephemeral appearance.

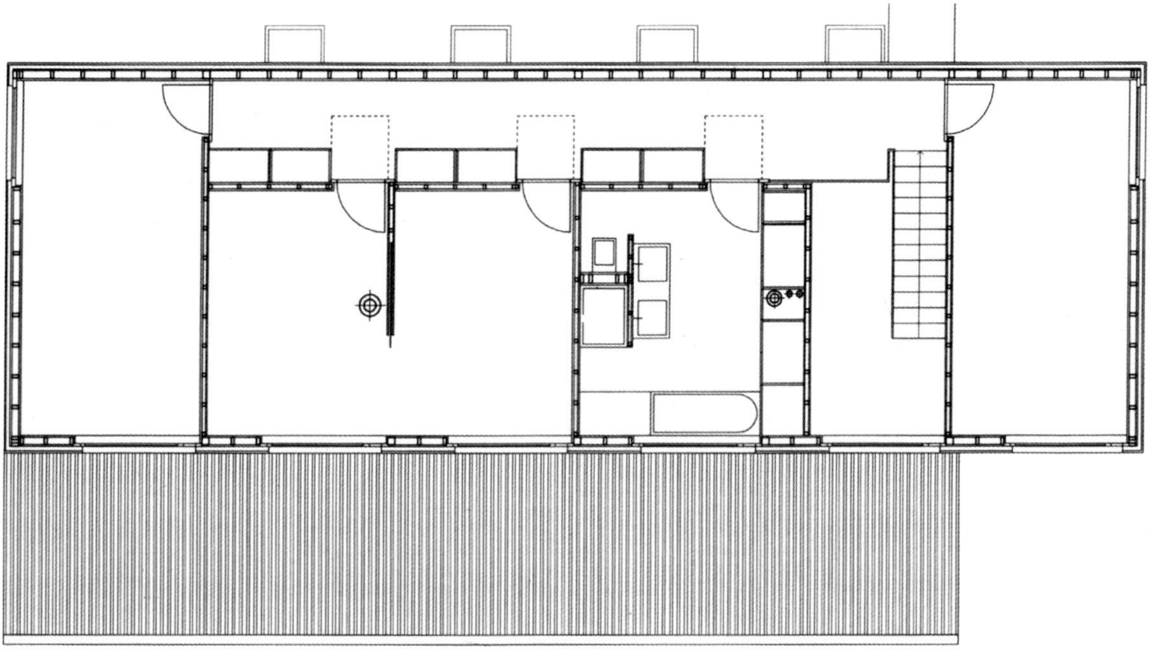

First floor plan

South elevation

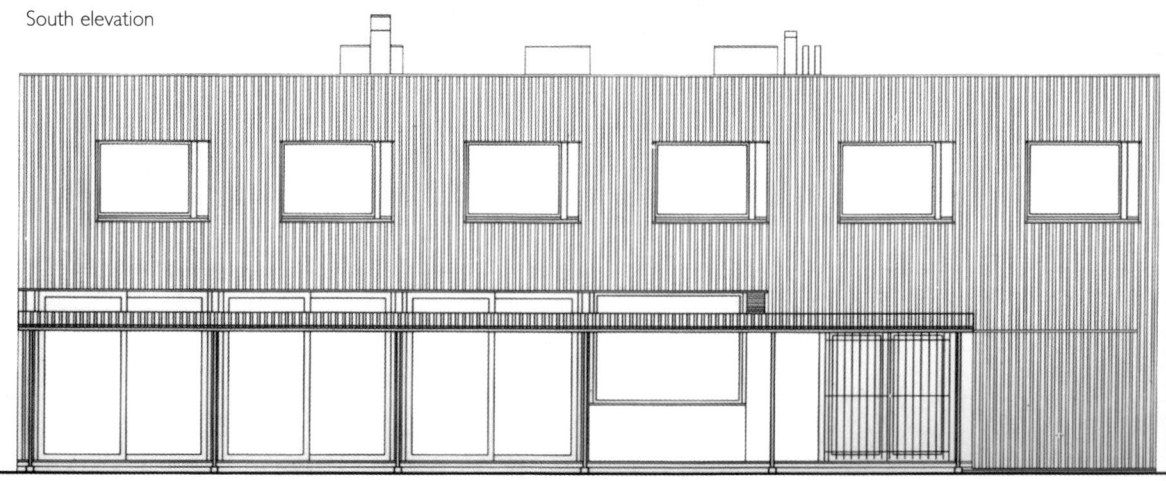

North elevation

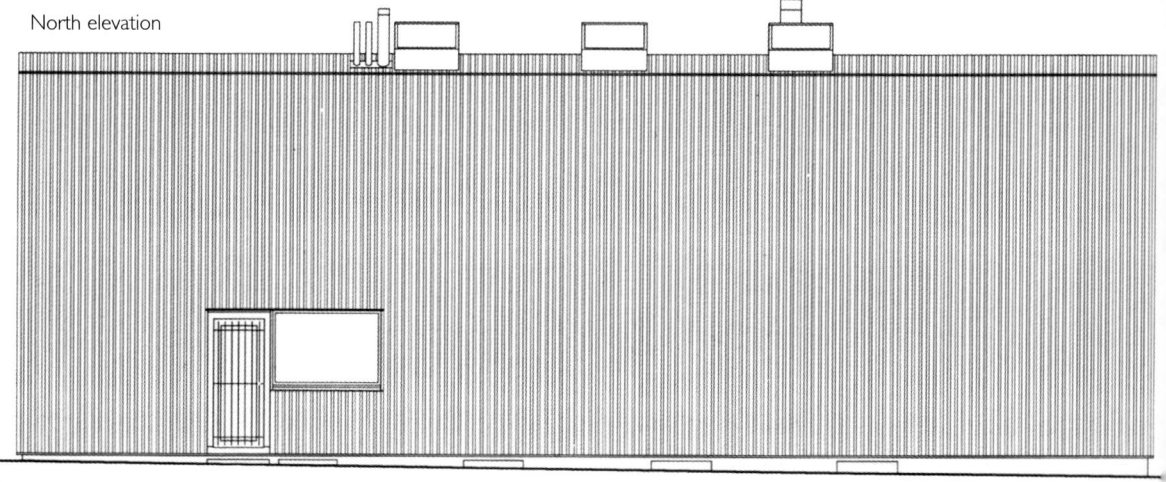

Cross section

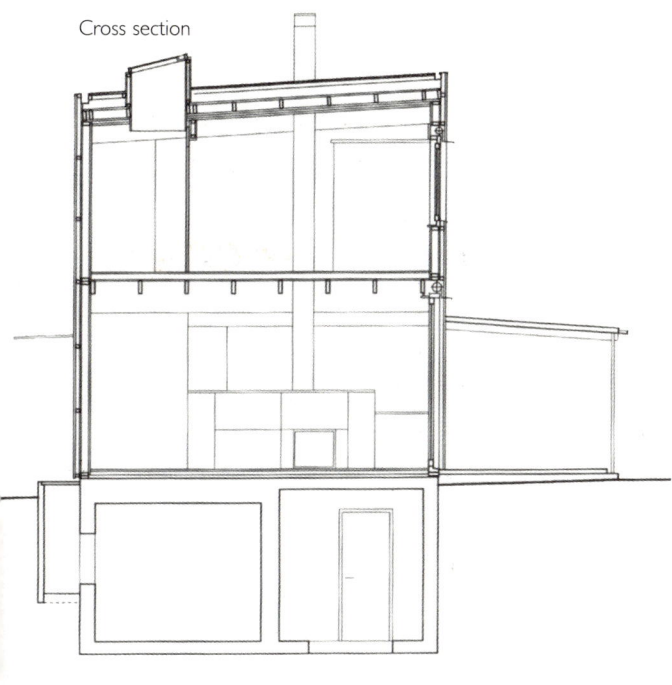

West elevation

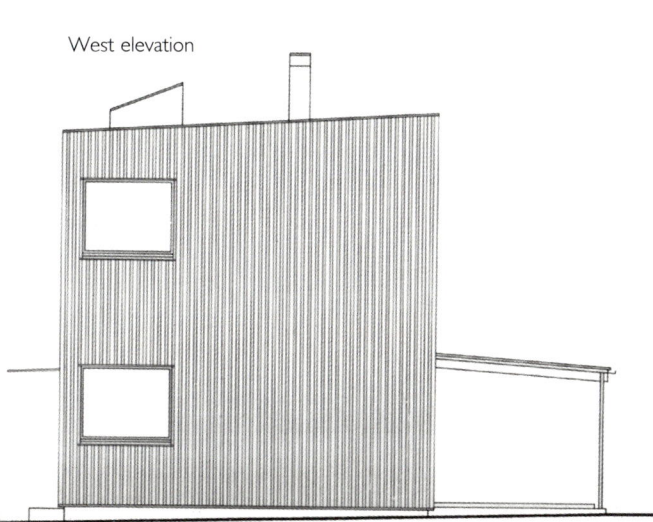

Behnisch & Partner

Charlotte House

Sillenbuch, Germany

Photographs: Behnisch & Partner, Christian Kandzia

The Charlotte house is almost an exception in the work of Behnisch & Partners, whose projects are normally of a greateer scope. However, in the design of this dwelling, they show a great knowledge of the architectural models of the past and great acuity in adapting them to the functional and environmental needs of the present. Indeed, the difficult problem facing them in this suburb of Stuttgart, with very high land prices, is similar to that faced by Adolf Loos in the design of the Horner hpuse in Vienna (1913): a very small plot on which the planning regulations drastically reduced the permitted ground plan.

In addition to the main dwelling, the programme was to include several rented apartments, although due to the planning regulations and the size of the plot only one was left in the final design. It was located on the top level inorder to provide intimacy and privacy for the different families that would live in the building. The Functional requirements called for the installation of a lift, and all the rooms had to have certain dimensions and receive a special treatment.

The most outstanding feature of the design is the vaulted roof, which provides a large habitable space and differentiates the building from its typological environment of dwellings with peaked roofs.

The house introduces radical innovations in its adaptation to the environmental requirements. The ecological intent of the design is seen both in the construction systems and in the selection of materials: paints and lacquers made from natural resins, wood that is not protected by chemical products, cellulose-based recyclable materials as an alternative to the habitual mineral fibre insulation... In the design of the smaller facades we can also see this attention to ecology and the environment: the south facade is open towards the street in order to take advantage of the light and solar energy, whereas the north facade is more closed to save energy and ensure privacy.

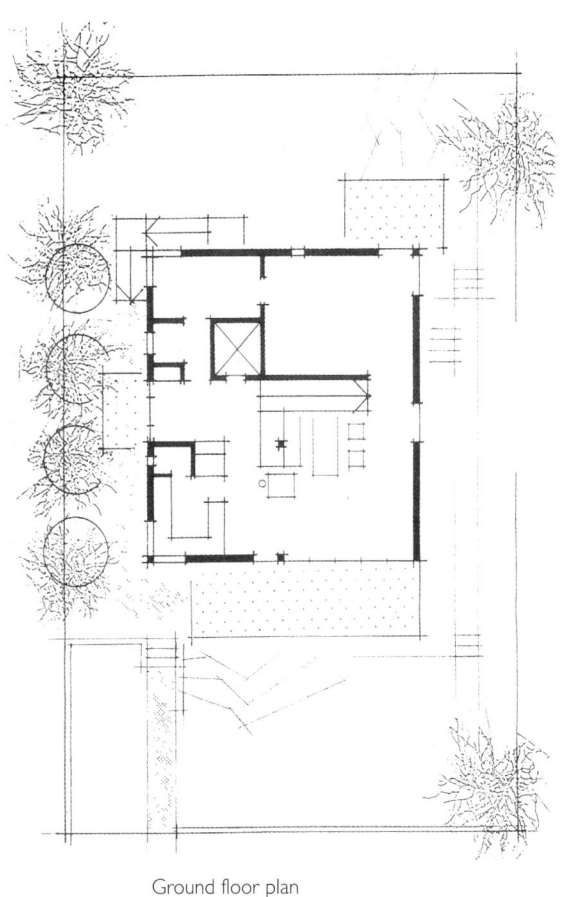

Ground floor plan

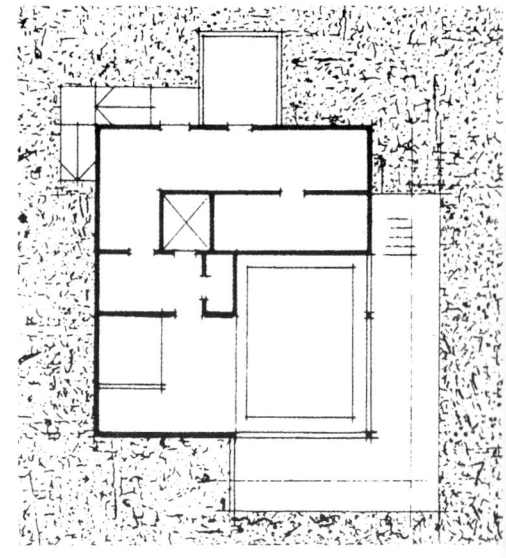

Basement floor plan

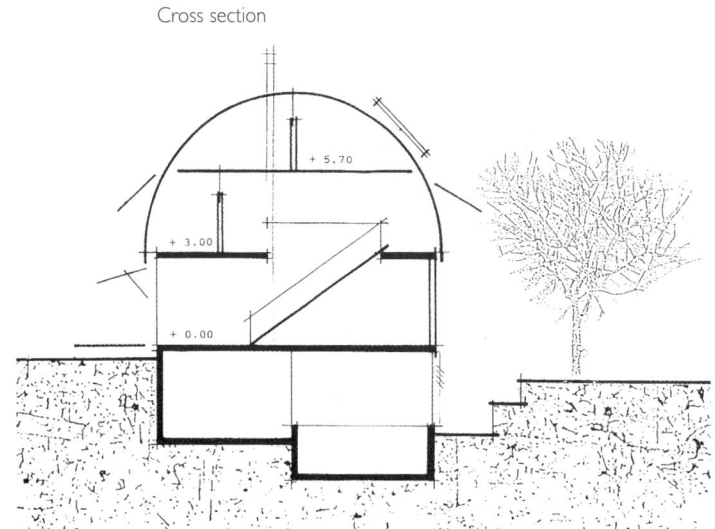

Cross section

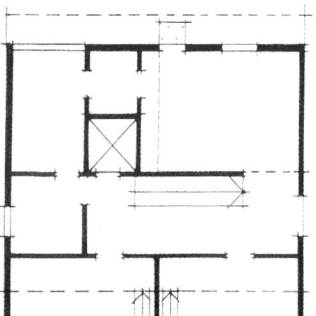

First floor plan

The plans, the section and the facades reveal the architectural solution to the problem of the small ground plan permitted by the planning regulations. It consists of a very compact and almost cubic volume (from basement to attic) that takes advantage of the sloping land to locate a semi-basement. The roof, which brings to mind a covered wagon, houses and apartment. The metal roof cladding bears a battery of solar panels.

We see careful relation to the most immediate surroundings: staircases and small terraces favour the independence of the different family groups that live in the building.

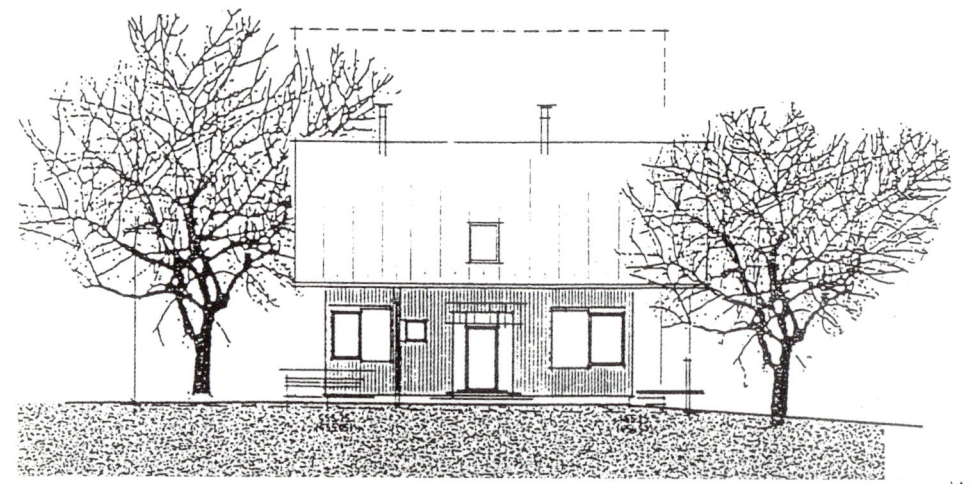

West elevation

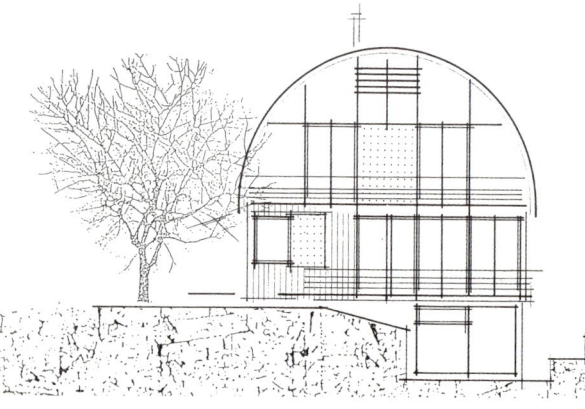

north elevation

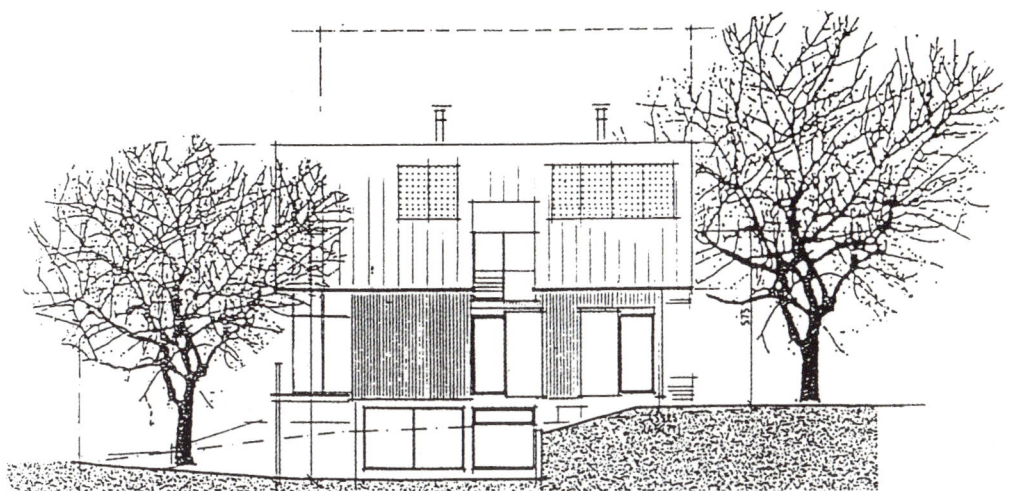

East elevation

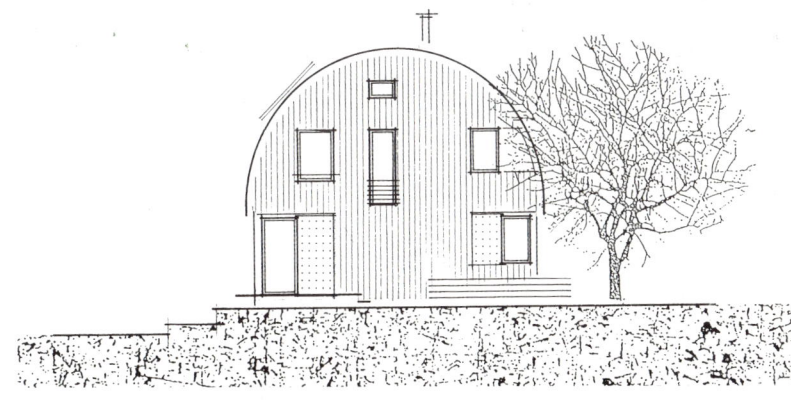

South elevation

123

LOG ID

Residential Building in the Black Forest

Schramberg, Germany

Photographs: Reiner Blunck

This home for a family of four is situated on a sloping plot, close to a preexisting detached house in Schramberg, in the Black Forest, overlooking the town and the castle. The aim of the architects was to build a solar house, including a separate apartment, which would complement the neighbouring house.

Access from the street above is over a footbridge in metal grating alongside the parking platform, which just out over the garden.

Solar architecture was a basic premise of the new building from the design stage, and is clearly discernible in the ground plan. The body of the construction, with outer walls in Poroton 36,5 cm thick, is compact in order to minimize its surface area and the resulting diffusion of heat.

Solar energy is collected passively in the 64-square-meter glasshouse, which faces southwest and is shaped to take full advantage of the sun as it crosses the sky. The heat thus generated is then used actively, being distributed throughout the 360 aquare meter of living space. The plants in the glasshouse also contribute to the health of the family by producing oxygen and bonding harmful substances.

Daylight enters through the glasshouse and also through a fanlight in the main body of the house. Beneath the fanlight, a glass reticular arrangement allows natural light to penetrate as far as the living room.

The glasshouse has a steel structure with thermal glass surfaces, while the interiors are in white mineral plaster for the walls and white marble for the floors.

The project is a successful example of how to combine environmentalism and high-quality detached housing.

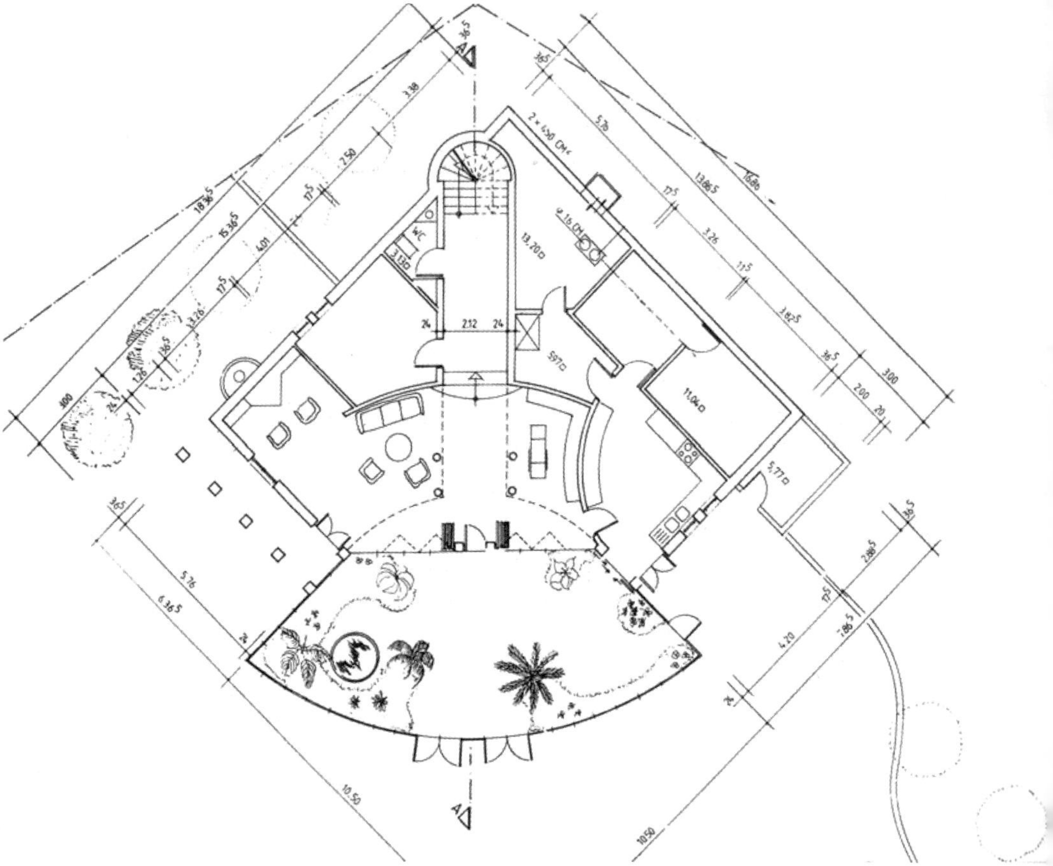

Ground floor

North elevation

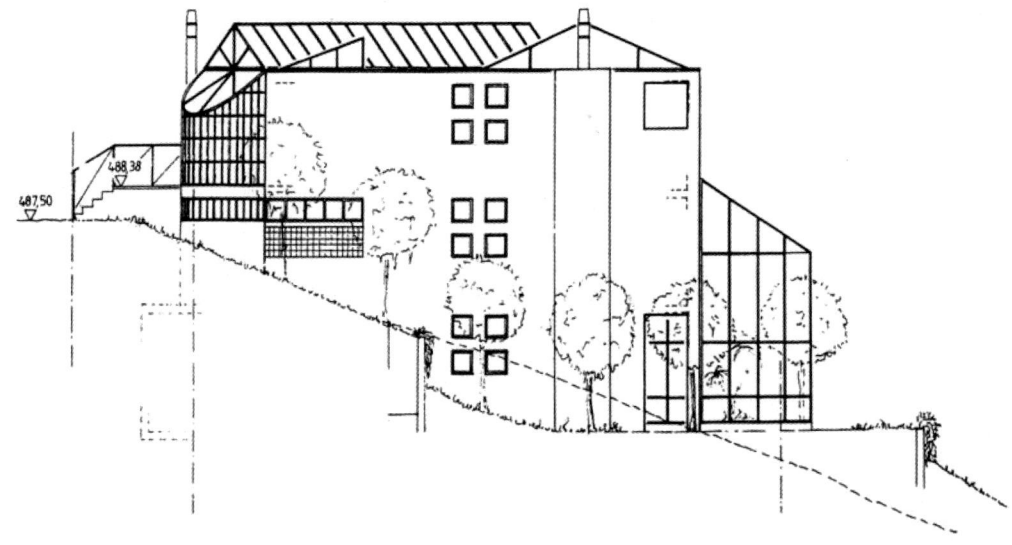

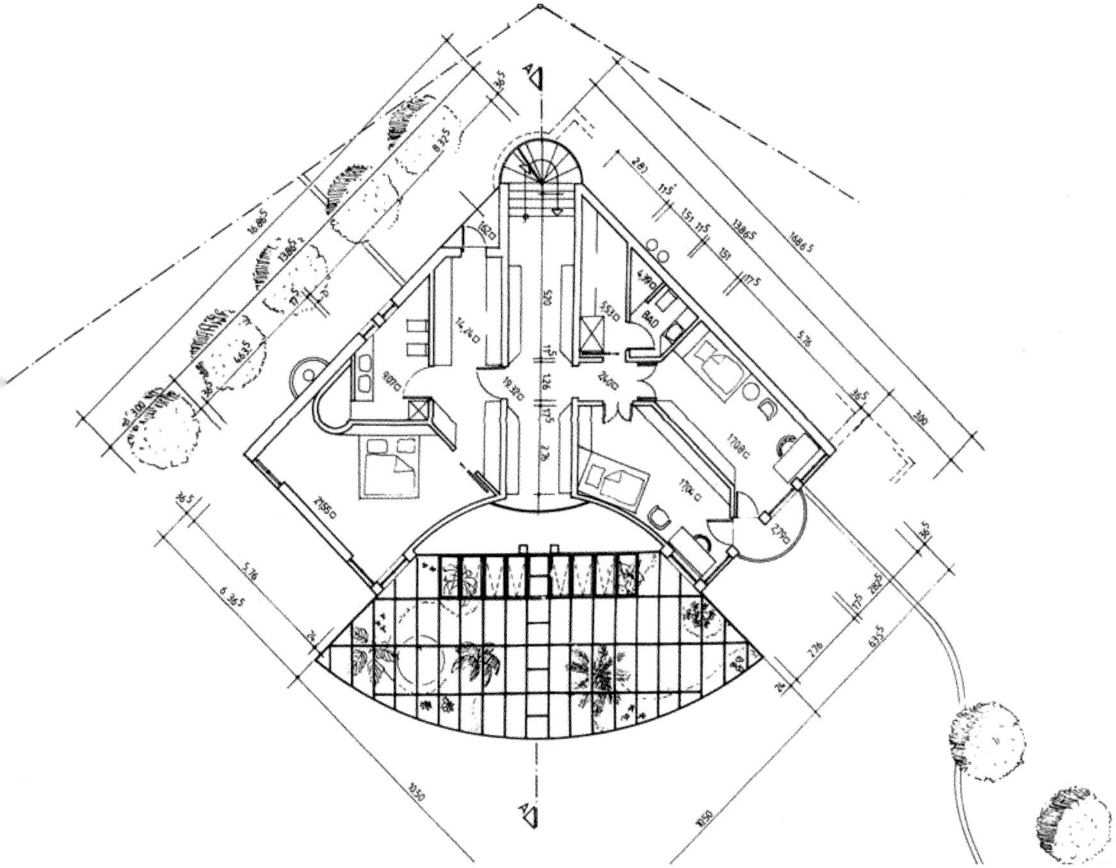

First floor plan

The design is typical of solar architecture, with minimal openings on the north, in contrast to the large glazed surfaces facing south.

South elevation

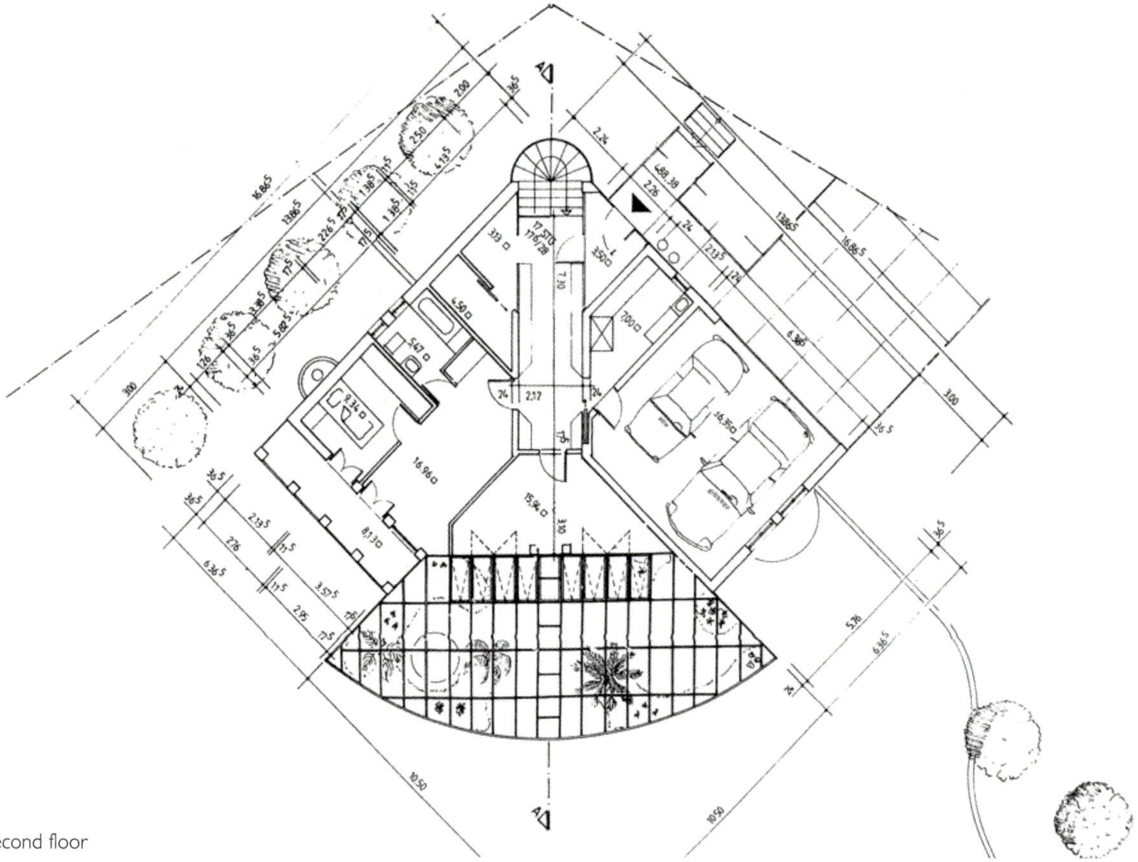

Second floor

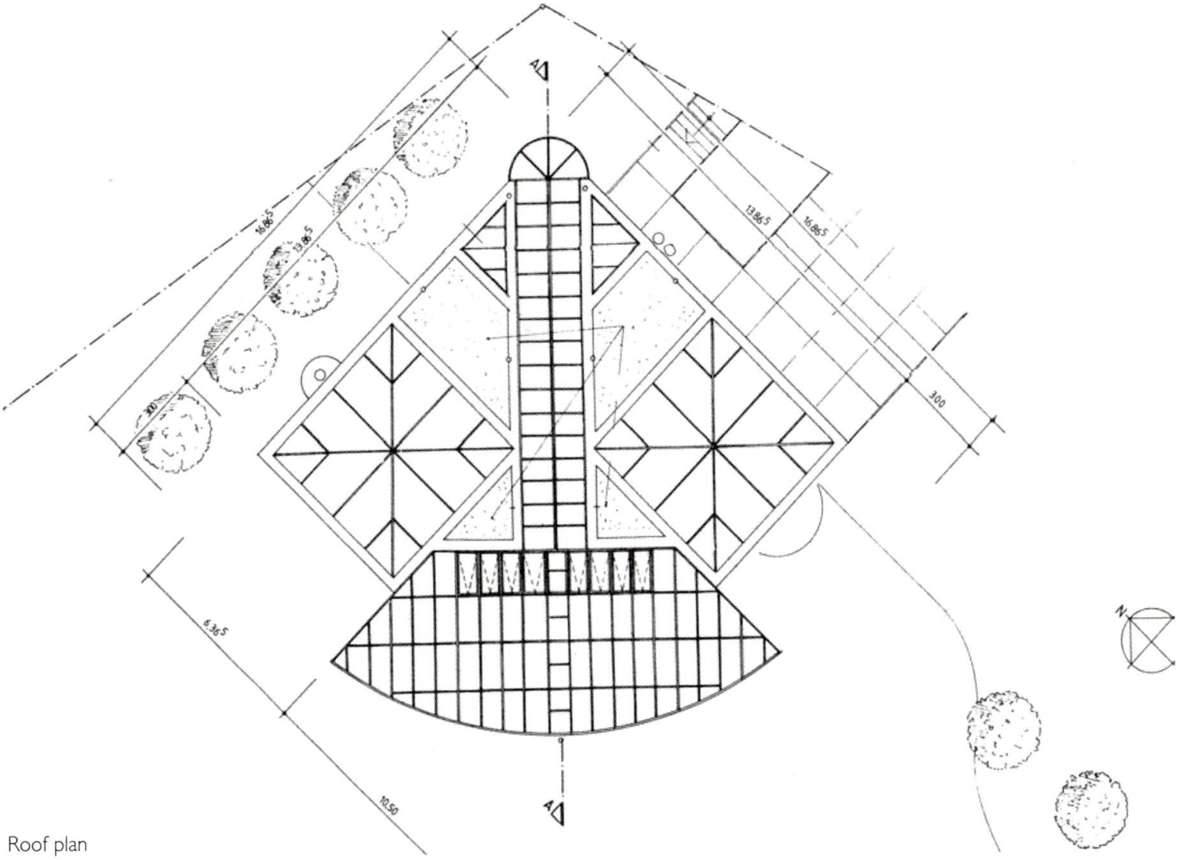

Roof plan

Light is diffused through the glass surfaces, creating a transparent space in which reflections are reinforced by the highly polished floor and the depth produced by the glass-floored landing above.

At night the house appears to be returning the energy it stored up during the day.

Mario Botta

House in Daro-Bellinzona

Daro, Switzerland

Photographs: Pino Musi

The architecture of Mario Botta is characterized by its formal power and the strong presence of its volumes. His buildings do not attempt to blend into their surroundings; rather, he aims to impose his architecture on them, to implant themselves with all the vigor of their architectural mass and become landmarks in the landscape. The home in Daro is a clear example of this. It is located in the Swiss canton of Ticino, but is not subordinated to its Alpine setting. Instead, it takes advantage of the relief of the site to emerge with force, seeking to make a plastic, expressive impact.

This home abstains from the expected Alpine typology and places all its visual power not in volume but in what amounts to a single facade, which acts as a formal and visual point of reference for the whole project. All the expressive force of the building is concentrated on this facade, and is formalized in a wall with a fragmented design. The wall, which includes the main entrance, is defined by two characteristic features: the singular arrangement of gray, square cement blocks, which produce an array of effects in the sunlight; and the transparent domed roof which crowns the building, giving it, in the words of Sergio Polano, the air of a "sun temple of an unknown civilization". From the starting point of this facade, the building is laid out volumetrically to form a three-story body reminiscent of the keel of a ship embedded in the ground. A fourth level, in the basement, makes use of the slope of the land to create an extension, which is used as the garage and service area.

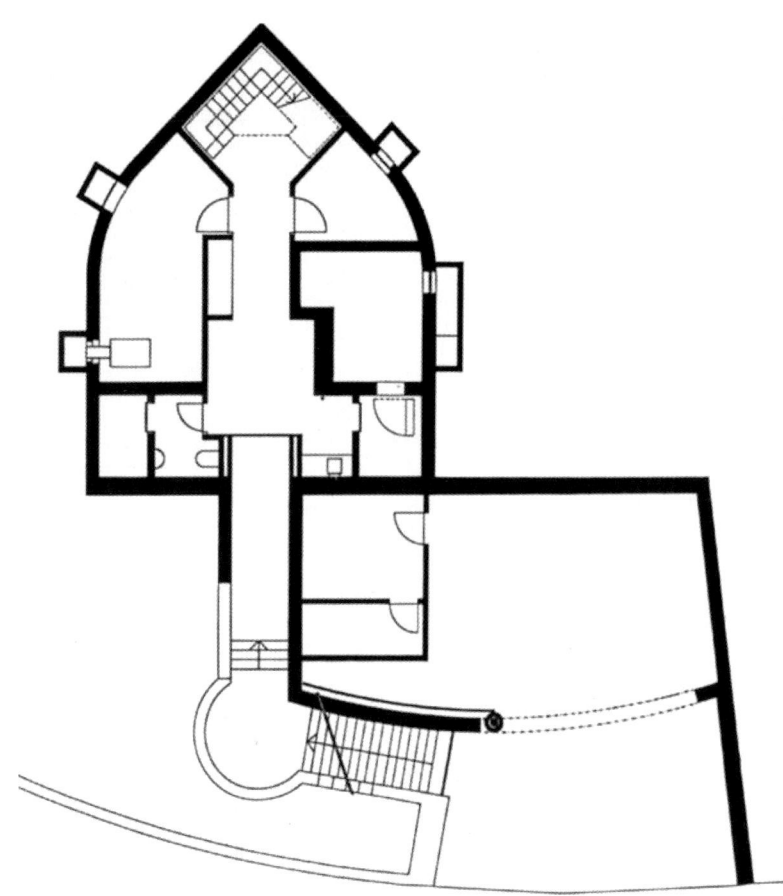

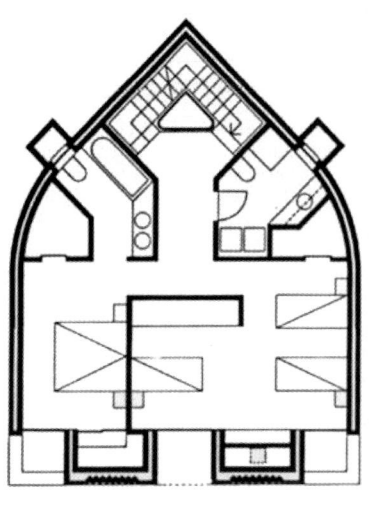

Ground floor plan

Basement floor plan

First floor plan

Secondo floor plan

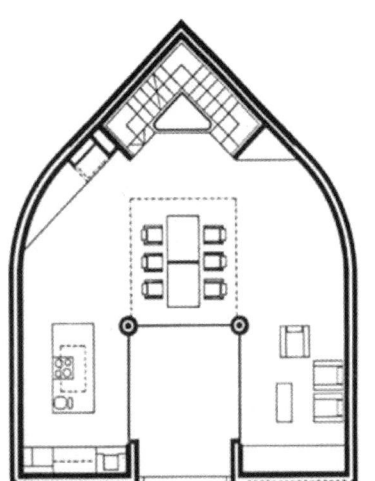

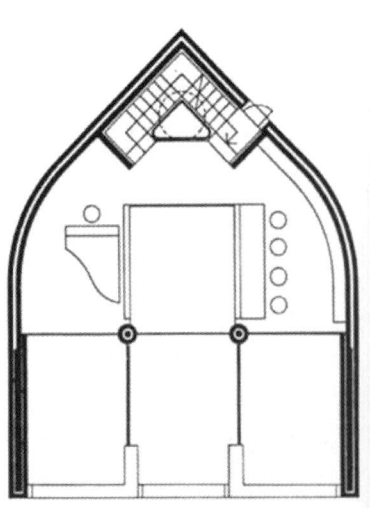

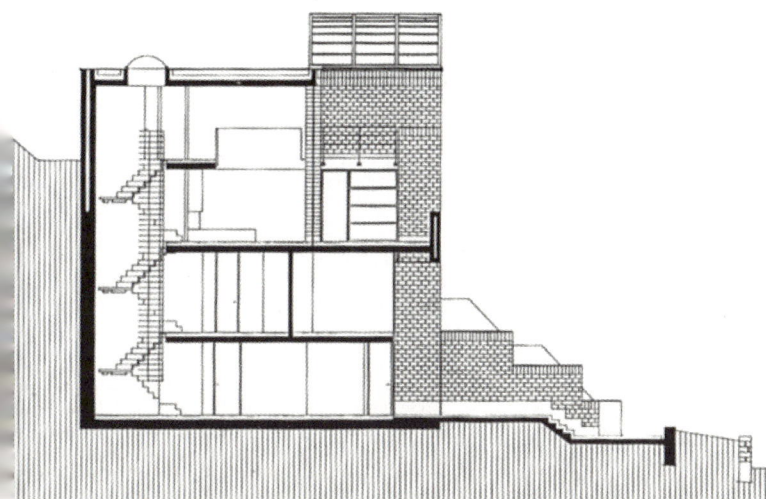

The main facade of the house in Daro imposes itself on the natural surroundings. Despite its rather hermetic, castle-like look the building opens up towards the landscape, and its transparent roof captures all the luminosity of the Alps.

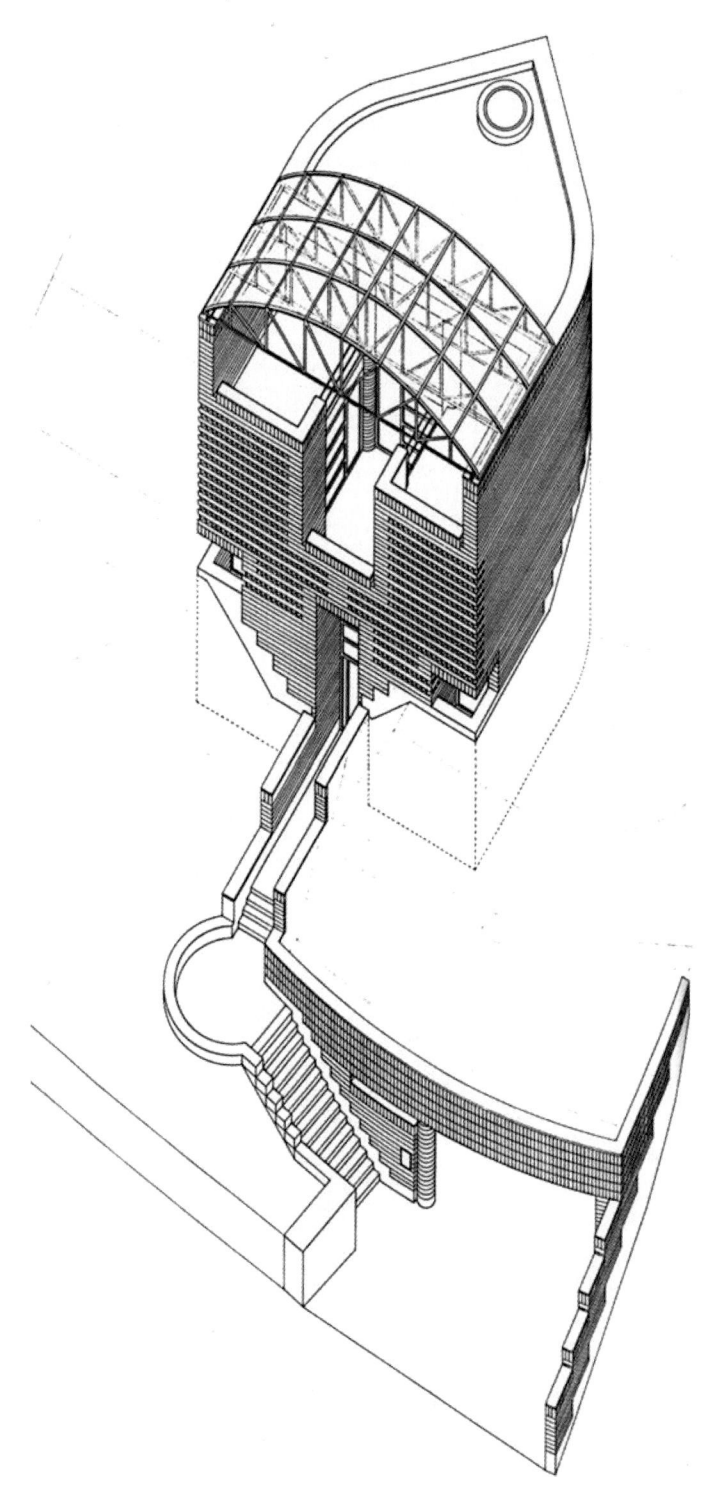

The transparent roof and the arrangement of the concrete blocks define the image of the main facade. The sleek lines of the metal fixtures provide unobstructed views throughout the interior.

Eduard Bru

Cabani House

Castellar de N'Hug, Spain

Photopgraphs: Jordi Bernadó, Eduard Bru

The design of this single family dwelling in Castellar de n'Hug (Barcelona province) was undertaken by Eduard Bru with the objective of enhancing the characteristics of the site and its primary asset, the pre-Pyrenean countryside. The house was built on an incline facing the landscape, situated so as to optimize the visual perspectives in the direction of the site's slope.

The ground plan was dictated by the relief. From the access, located on the upper level, the building is arranged on two floors as far as the unevenness of the terrain permits.

Both floors, in spite of their relentless search for a relation with the countryside, present distinct layouts. The lower, more conditioned by the terrain, houses the library and garage. The upper, where the living areas are located, enjoys freer planning and is more daring in its relation to the surroundings, culminating in a terrace open to the landscape.

The volumetric conception has also been molded to the terrain and to the idea of enhancing visual perspectives. This explains the soft curvature of the facades: in the eastern elevation, the inflection is marked by a vertical glazed border, which incorporates a contrasting element in the essentially opaque surface. Finally, the selection of materials is in consonance with the typological context and standards: stone-masonry walls (with two varieties characteristic of the site) and restored local tile.

The interior materials are differentiated by level. On the ground floor they are more natural with stronger textures suitable for resisting direct contact with the terrain; on the upper floor, they are lighter and more neutral so as to not obstruct the relationship with the landscape. The tension of the curvature allowed for the creation of various wall layers, which differentiate the distinct spaces.

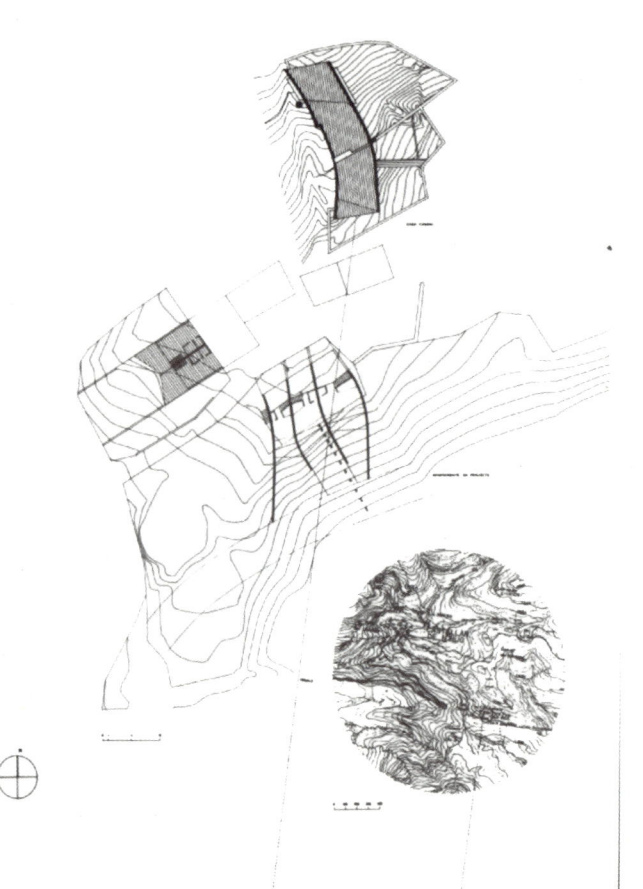

Ground floor plan

First floor plan

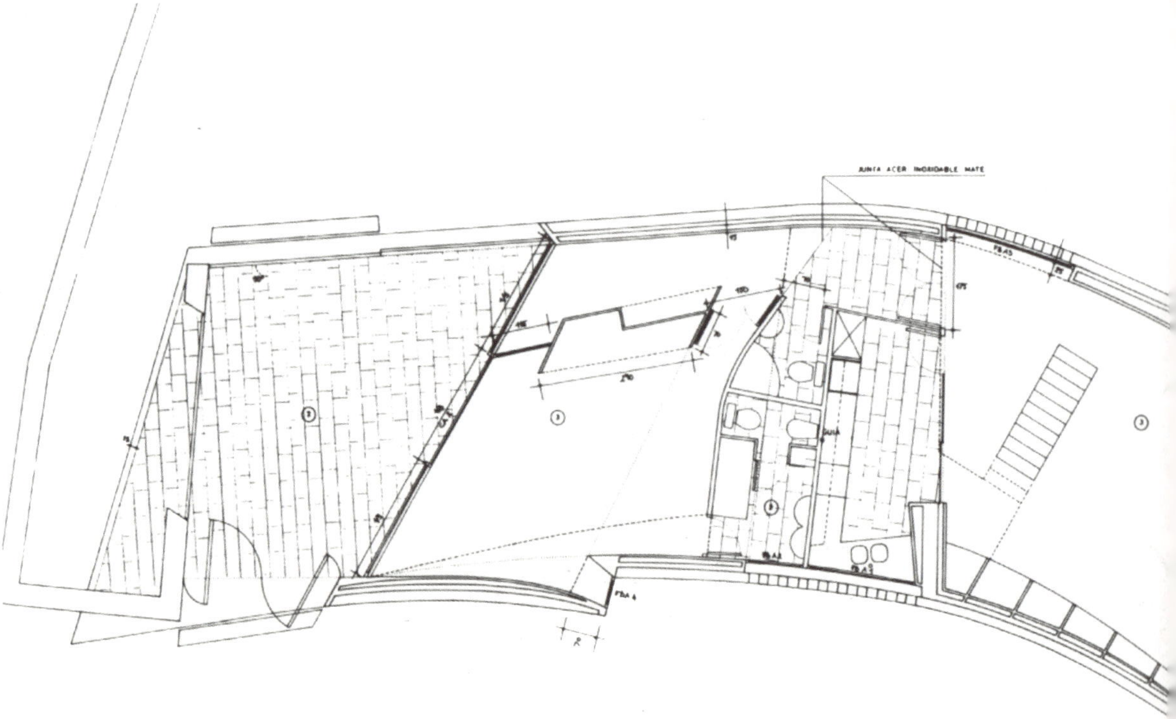

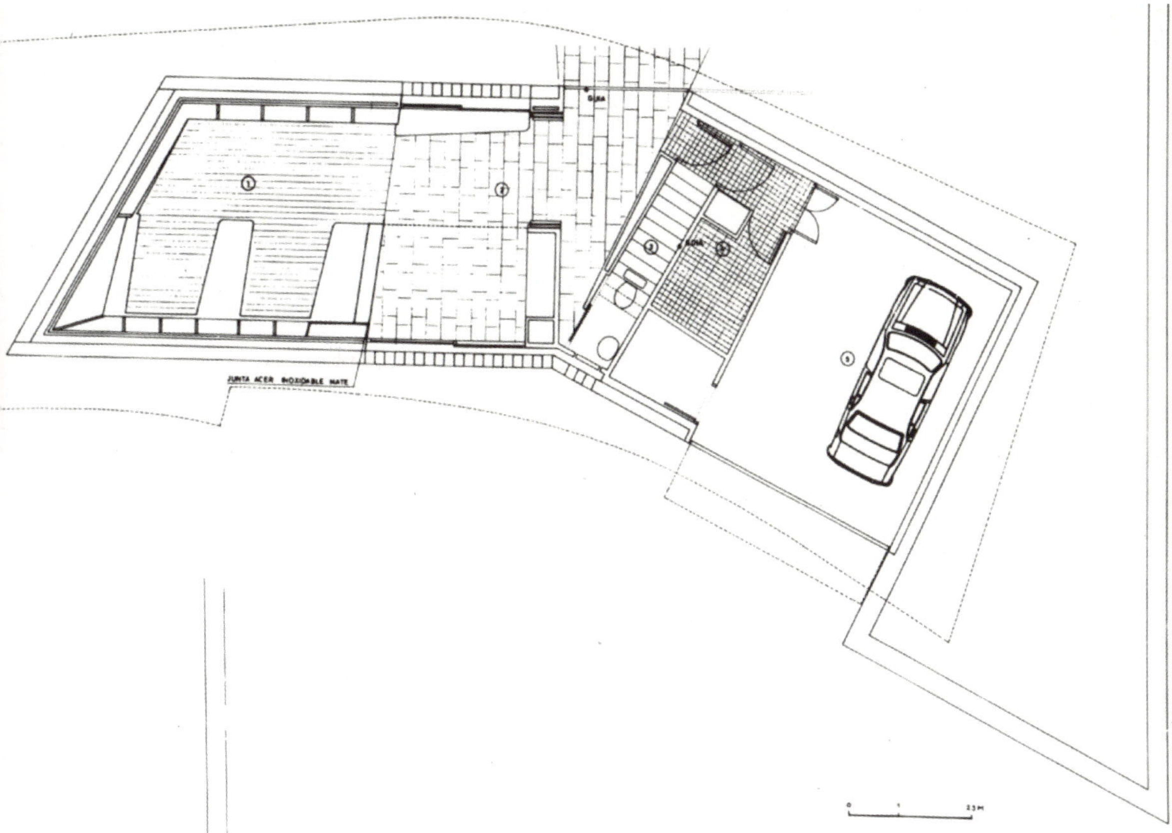
JUNTA ACER INOXIDABLE MATE

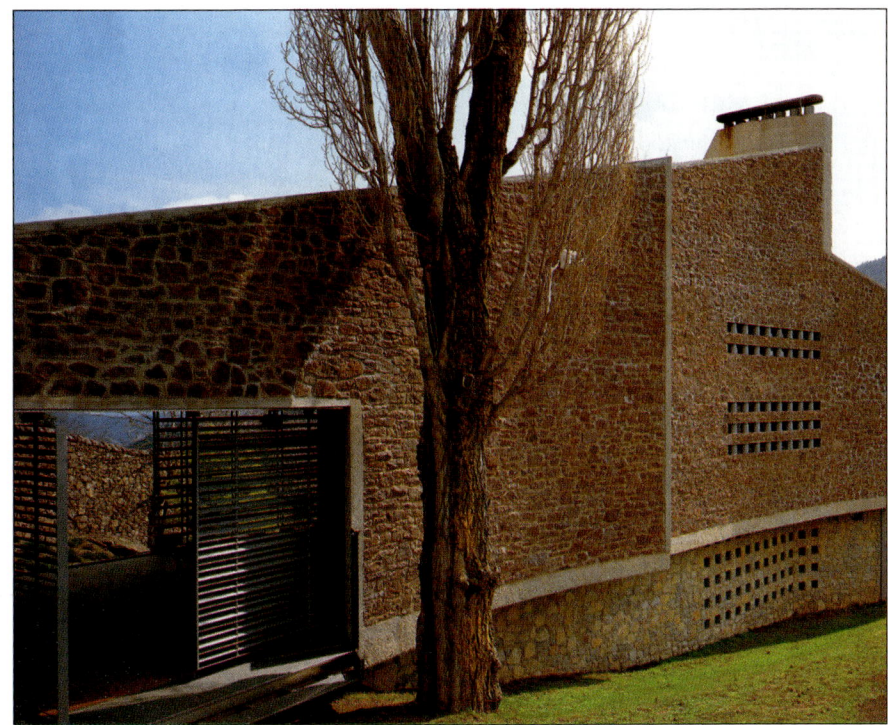

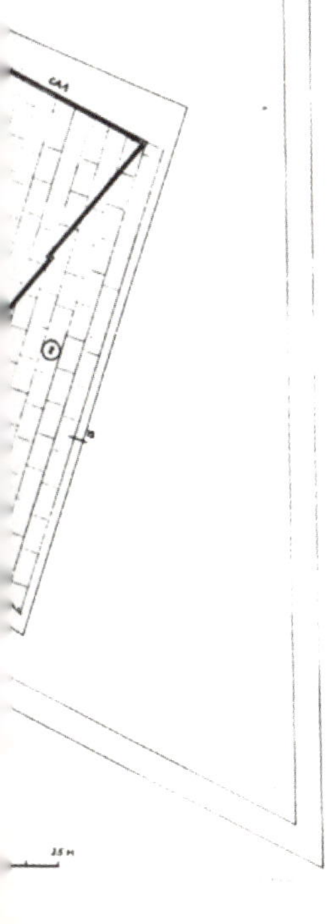

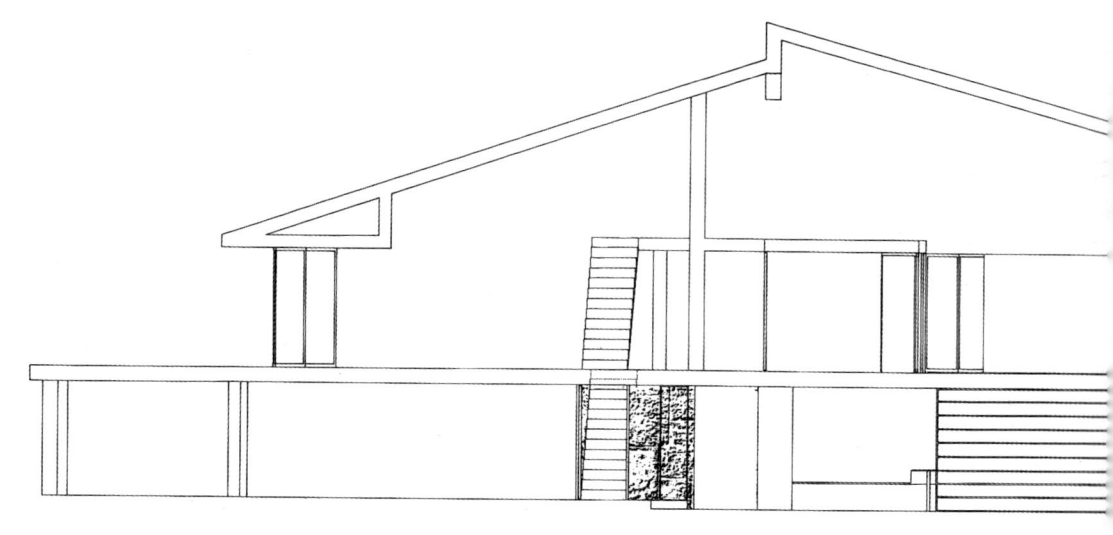
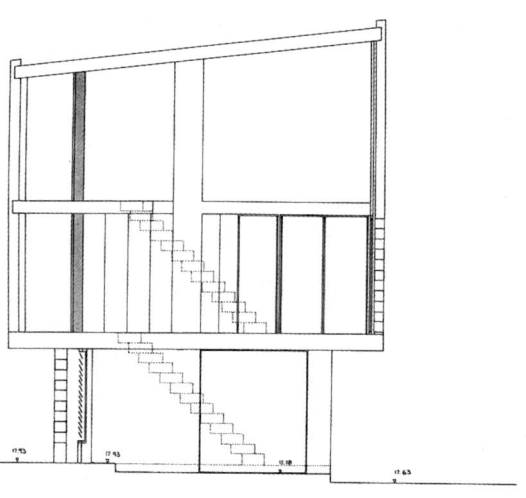
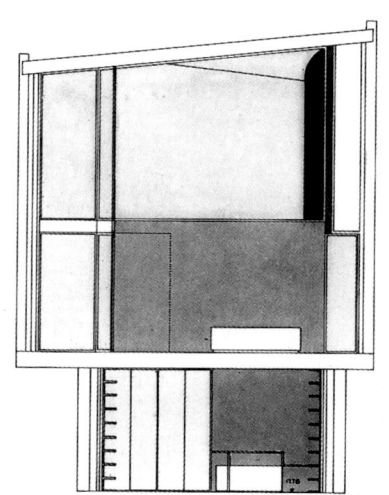

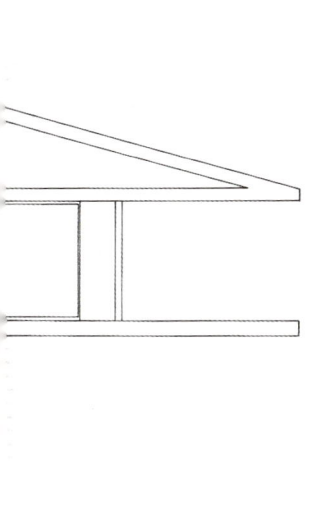

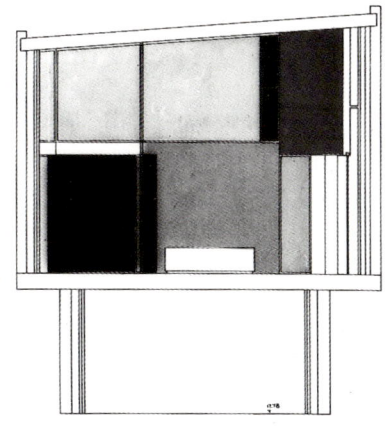

151

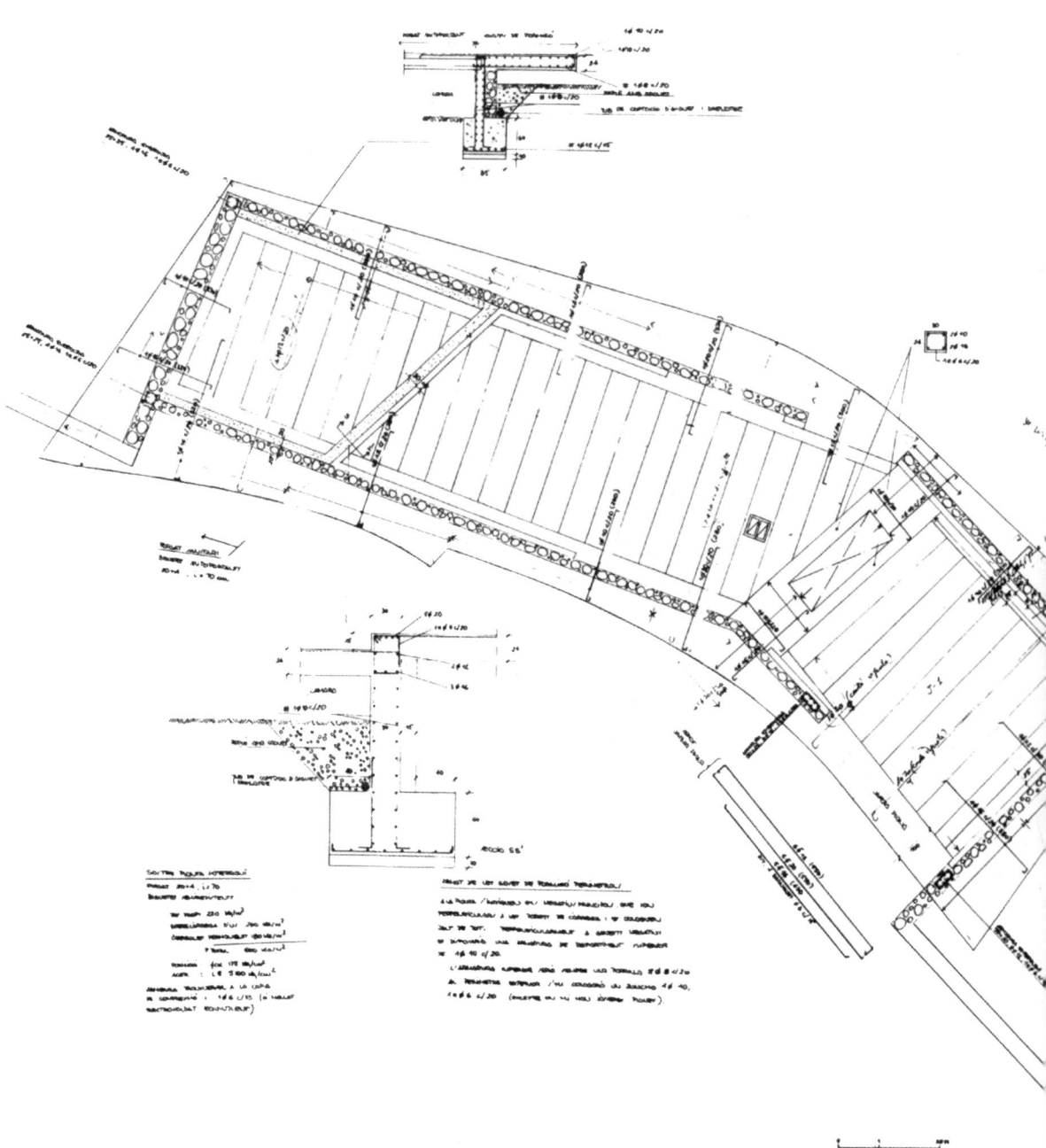

Daniel Calatayud

Calatayud House

Mont-Ras, Spain

Photographs: Daniel Calatayud

The architect Daniel Calatayud planned this home under the commission of his parents who owned a plot in Mont-Ras, in the province of Gerona. The site includes the ruins of a 10th century lookout tower, which is an important part of the town's heritage.

Two parameters guided the plan: on one hand, adaptation to the setting - both physical (relief and conservation of the woodland) and historical (the tower as a focal point), and on the other hand, an approach to architecture reminiscent of the 1930s, based on the use of high-quality materials, the direct relation between the construction crew and the architect and maximum attention to detail, which extends to the interior decoration and furnishings as well.

The tower served as a ordered element in the program. The access zone was built at the same level as the tower and split to create two parking areas: one to the south, sunken, for winter use, the other at the northern end, uncovered, for daily use. The tower also defined a central courtyard around which the two bodies were created. The home, enjoying views of the sea, lies in the south sector and has two levels, one of which is partially underground and houses the bedrooms. To the north, the annex serves to protect the courtyard and swimming pool from the strong north wind.

The project's unity is achieved thanks to a treatment of the material which follows the physical continuity between interior and exterior, especially in the flooring, roofs and modulation of the openings. With respect to the exterior language, the courtyard has been resolved through a terracing of crossbeams adapted to the slope of the land and a selection of local plant species. Fluidity of the spaces in the interior has been achieved through the elimination of doors, the incorporation of the baths in the bedrooms and the use of built-in furniture. The spaces are characterized by the furniture itself and the alternation of materials and colors.

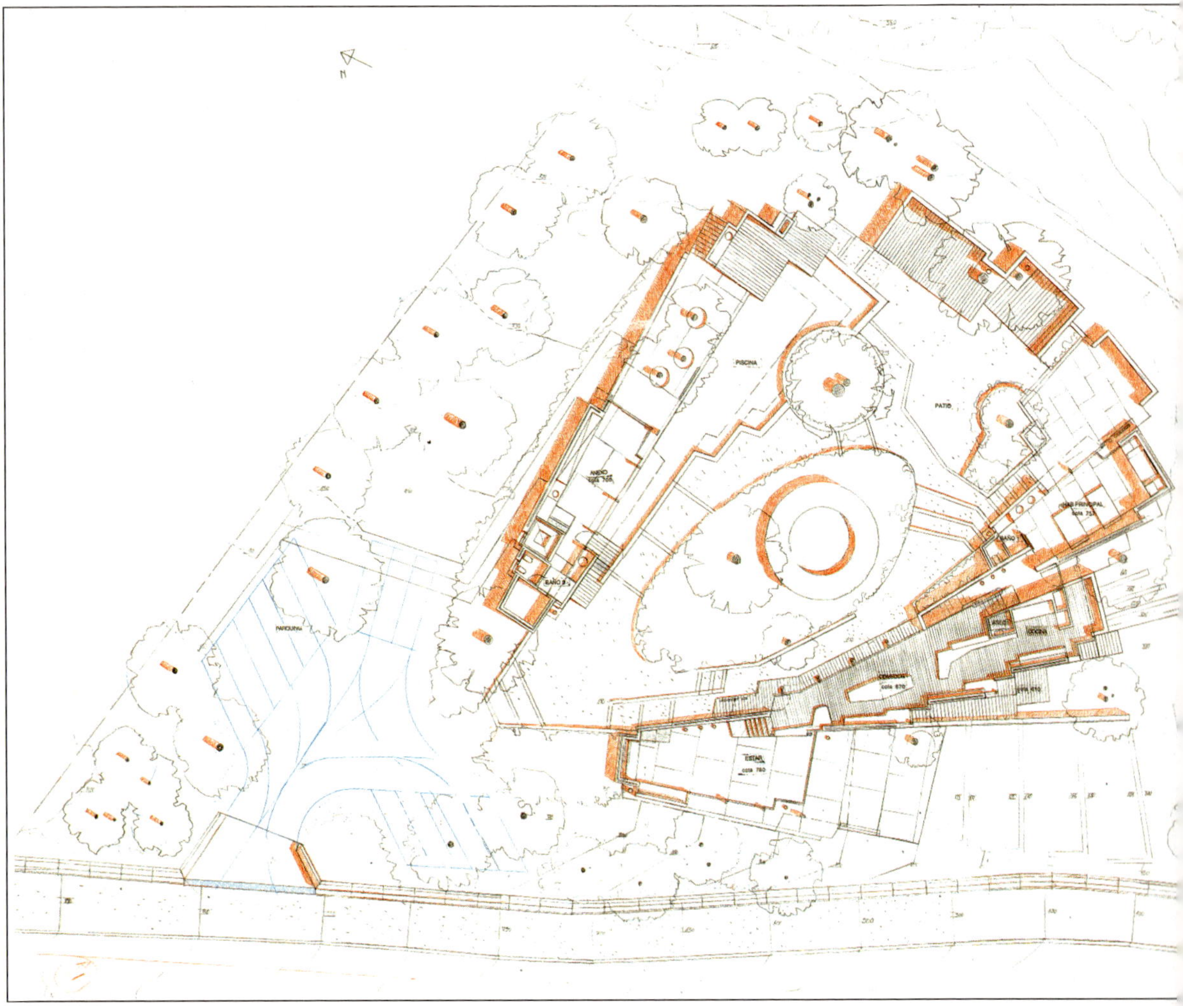
PISCINA
PATIO
COCINA
ESTAR

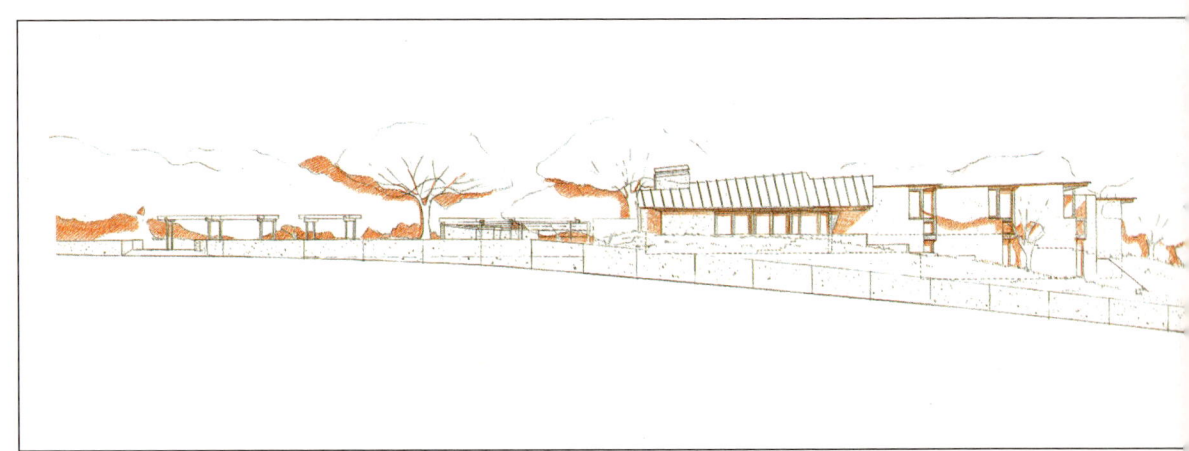

Genius loci. The remains of an ancient tower bear witness to the history of the site; imagining its original height of 56 feet, one can reconstruct the view of the corridor down which Charlemagne's armies marched.

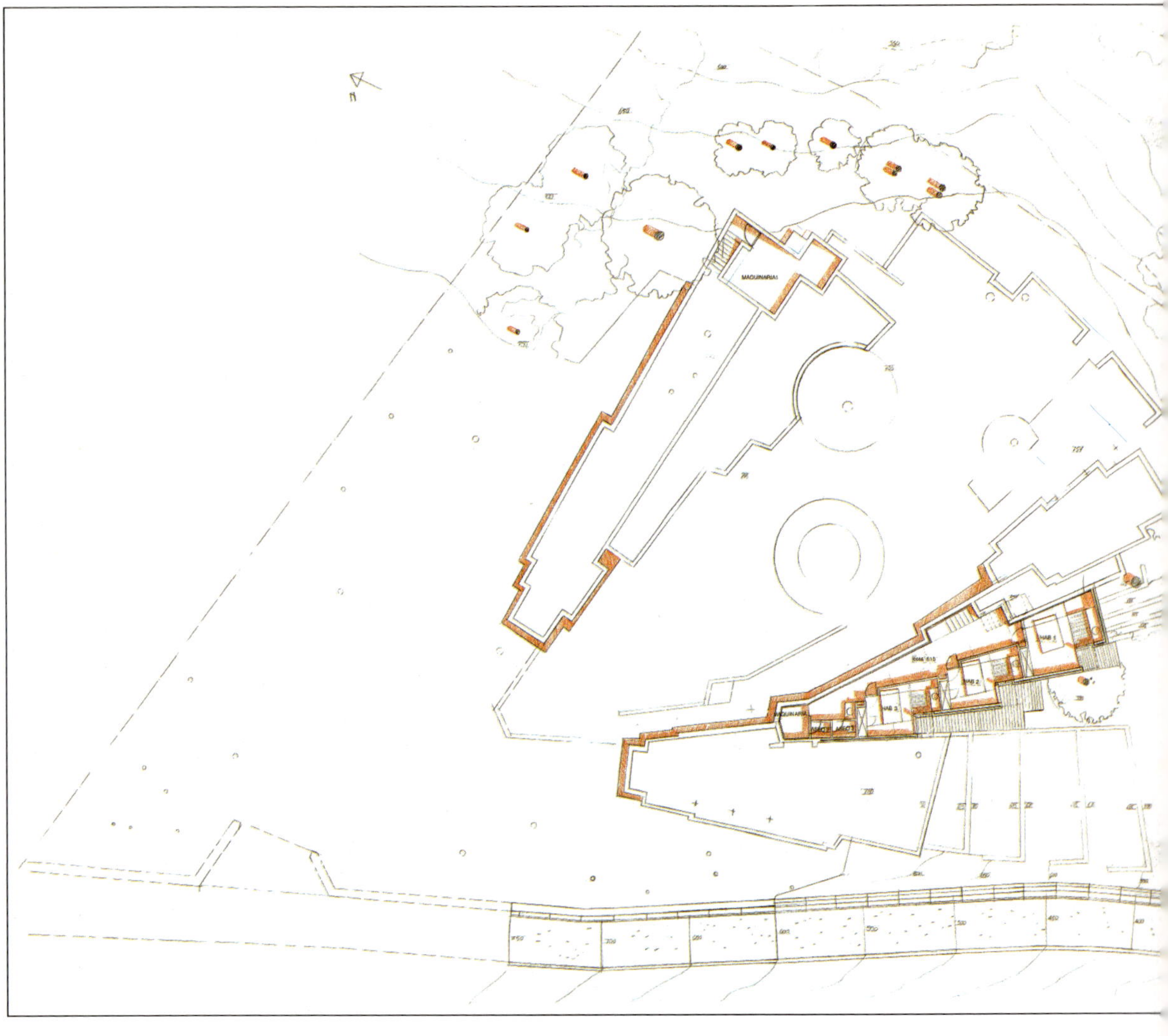
MAQUINARIA
HAB 1
HAB 2
HAB 3
MAQUINARIA

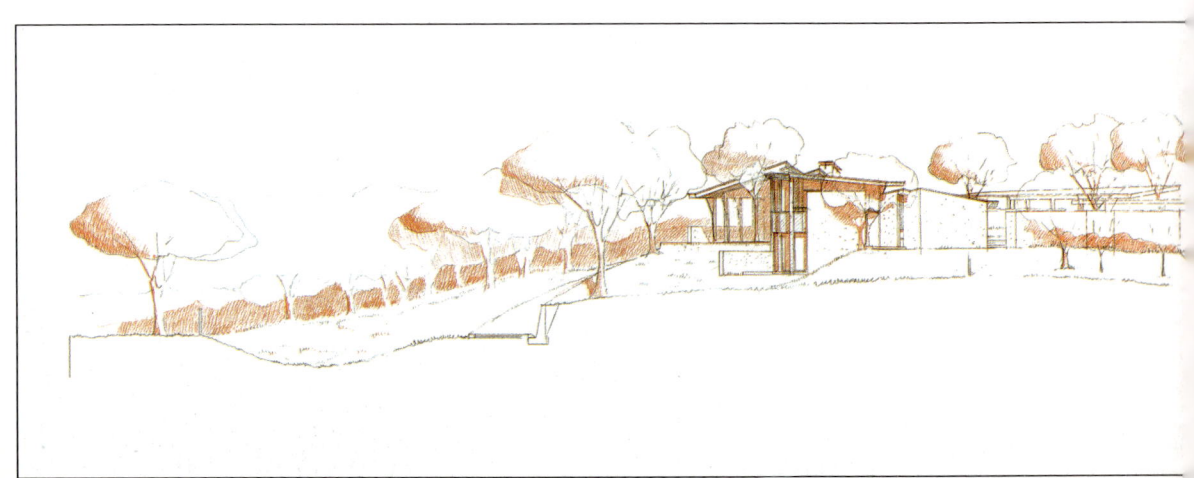

Integration and geometry: the elements of the site -ruins, relief, trees, views- generate an organic architecture.

Panoramic view of the volumes enclosing the central courtyard built around the tenth-century watchtower.

The swimming pool was designed in such a way as to respect the outcrop of rock and the existing holm oak.

Fluidity of space is achieved by extending the indoor flooring outdoors. The outside wall is conceived as a totally mobile element allowing the circulation of the sea breeze in the summer. Many of the furnishings are built into the walls; all are reduced to a minimum expression.

Per Line

House in Bryne

Bryne, Norway

Photographs: Per Line

This house can best be described as a fortification against the forces of nature. Its design is inspired by local vernacular architecture, which is a response to the harshness of the climate in this region. The undulating landscape in Jaeren, at the southwestern tip of Norway, was formed by the moraine deposited by the glacier that covered the Scandinavian Peninsula more than 10,000 years ago. The local climate is wet and windy, but mild in comparison with the rest of the country.

Both the house and the garage are built in load-bearing external timber stud walls over a concrete foundation, and walls and roofs alike are clad in tarred timber.

The weathered look of the external walls contrasts sharply with the rich yellow of the window frames, which carries over into the warm colors and materials of the interior living space. This is centered around a red brick fireplace and features pineboard floors and ceilings and painted fiberboard on the walls.

Although the house stands out from neighboring constructions, this is undoubtedly the most logical way to build in this area. It is conceived both as protection for its inhabitants against the weather and as a pleasant, cozy interior environment. It forms a sort of bird's nest around an atrium, thus creating a microclimate, which makes it comfortable to be outside. Furthermore, full advantage is taken of the available sunlight, with the garage on the northern side and picture windows on the south.

Ground floor plan

South elevation sud

1. Living & TV room
2. Laundry room
3. Storeroom
4. Leisure room
5. Bedroom
6. Dining room
7. Kitchen
8. Atrium
9. Garage

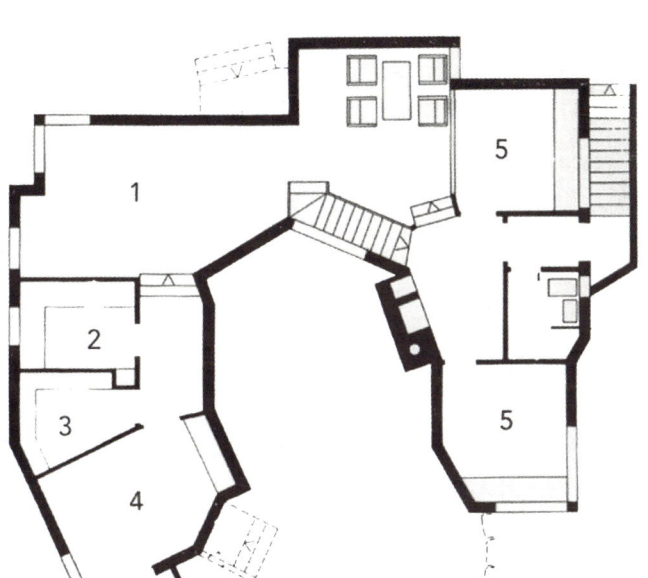

Basement floor plan

West elevation

The house folds in on itself in a crescent shape that forms an interior yard protected from, yet open to, the landscape. In order to facilitate maintenance, blend in with local traditional building styles and provide high thermal efficiency, wood is used for walls and roofs alike.

North elevation

East elevation

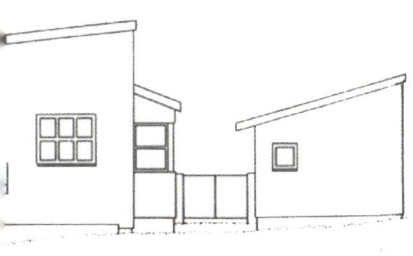

Roof plan

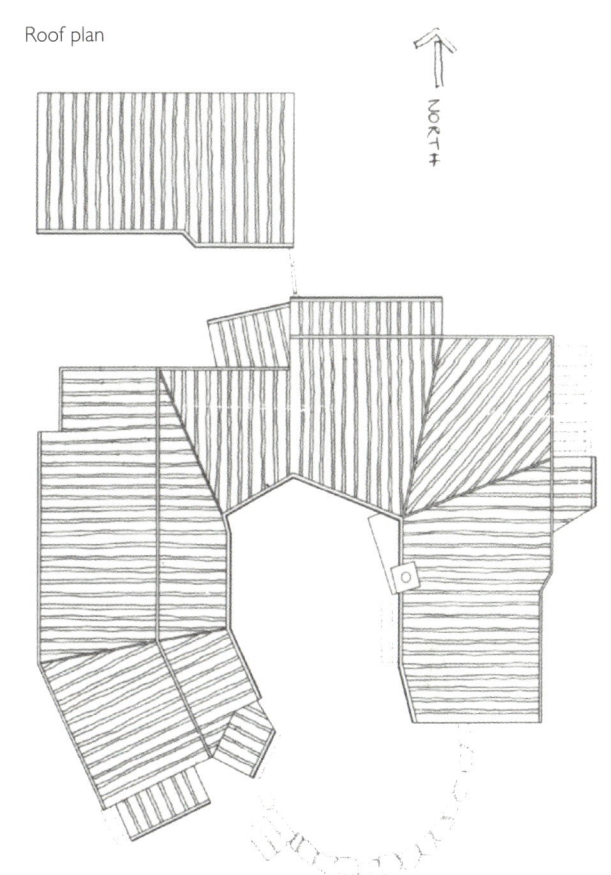

Warm and cold light: the house seems to live with the rhythm of the seasons in empathy with the surrounding nature.

The architect likes to compare this house to a nest: the layout of the rooms and the high profile given to wood and brick create an intimate, warm haven far removed from the damp and strong winds outside.

Göran Westman GWSK Arkitekter

Nyström House

Täby, Sweden

Photographs: Göran Westman GWSK Arkitekter

The lot is situated on the boundary between an old garden and the forest. A wall in the center of the house has been placed along this boundary, dividing the house into two parts: the northern private part, protected by the forest, and the living areas, facing south. Duality symbolizes the character of the house: on one side, a small traditional sector faces the forest, and on the other side, a more modern and generously open part faces the garden. The shape of the house in relation to the garden is of Japanese inspiration.

The extended plan of the house facilitates a division, making it possible to create a private space, now used by the children and with a possible future use as a small separate apartment for members of the extended family. The clients themselves wanted this double function, and also a traditional house but with some modern aspects. A factor that had to be considered was that the site had to be approached from the south. To ensure privacy and mark the limits of the courtyard, a garage/workshop was placed at the southern entrance. This also leads the visitor to the entrance on the north side of the house. The entrance hall is narrow to give direct contact with the garden and to integrate the house into nature. Except for a few steel columns the house is constructed of wood and has a sheet metal roof. There is a basement under the elevated part of the house and an attic is situated above the entrance and the children's rooms.

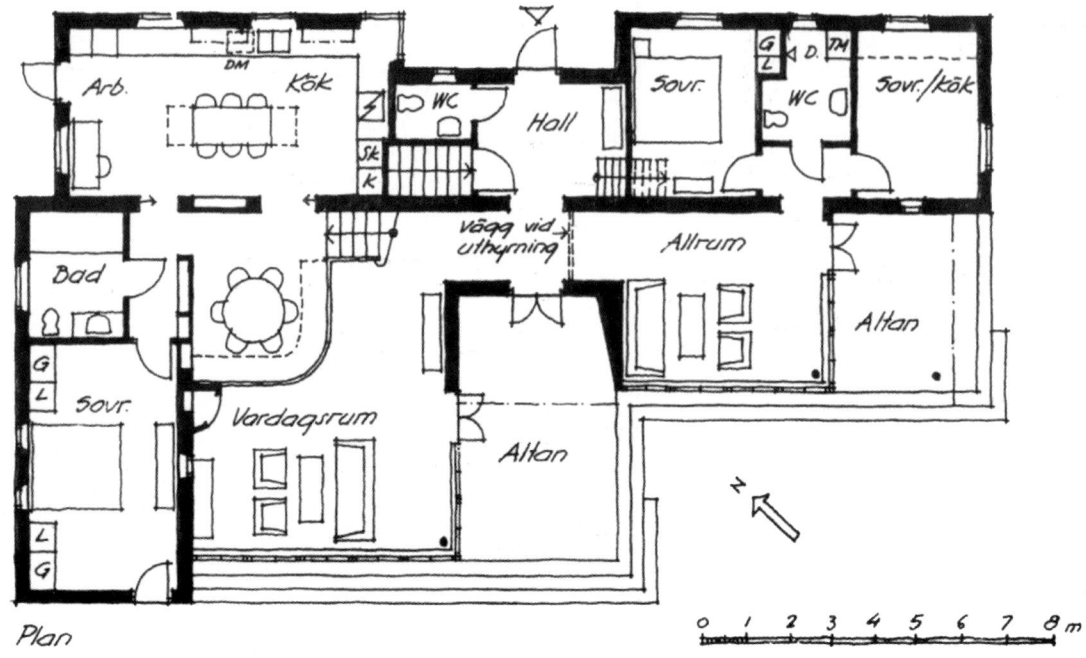

Plan

Ground floor plan

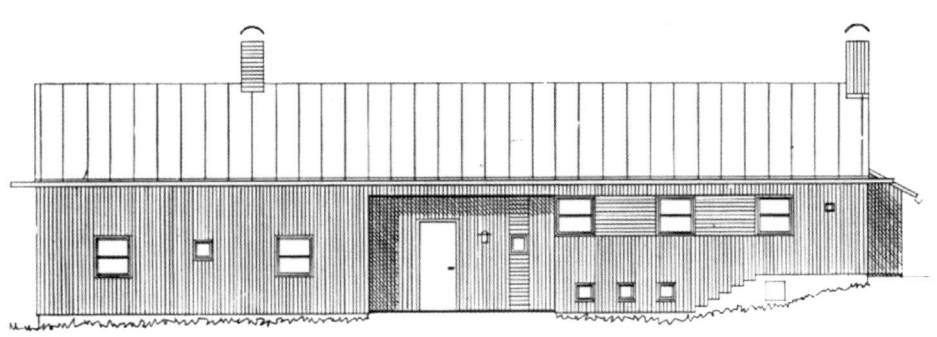

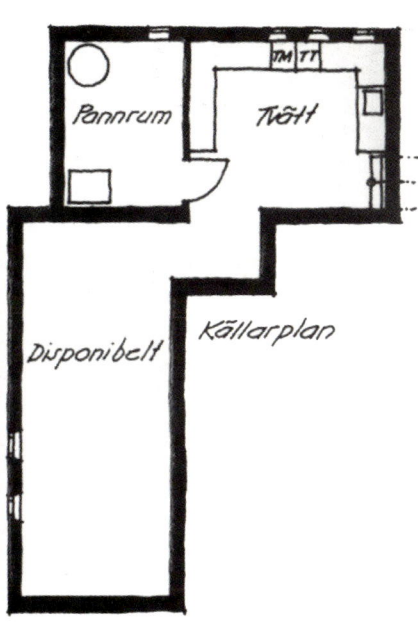

First floor plan

The luminosity of the construction stands out in the midst of the surrounding forest vegetation.

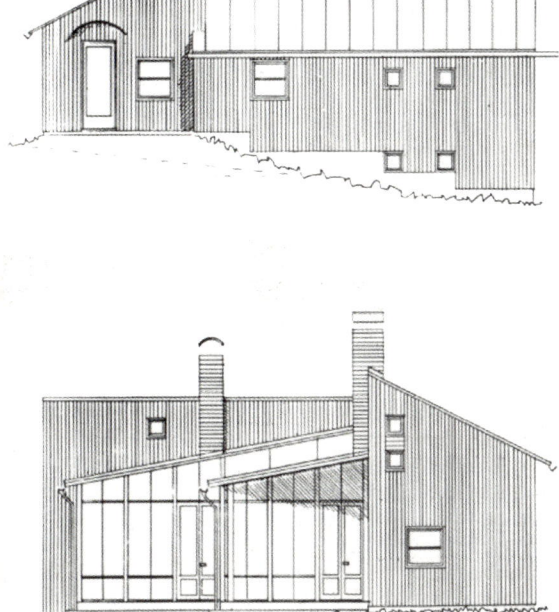

The concept of the house: a division into two parts, one of them more traditional and closed to the north on the forest side, the other more modern and open to the south on the garden side. The elongated plan shows another division into two with the creation of a space for the children, which may be comfortably used by future generations.

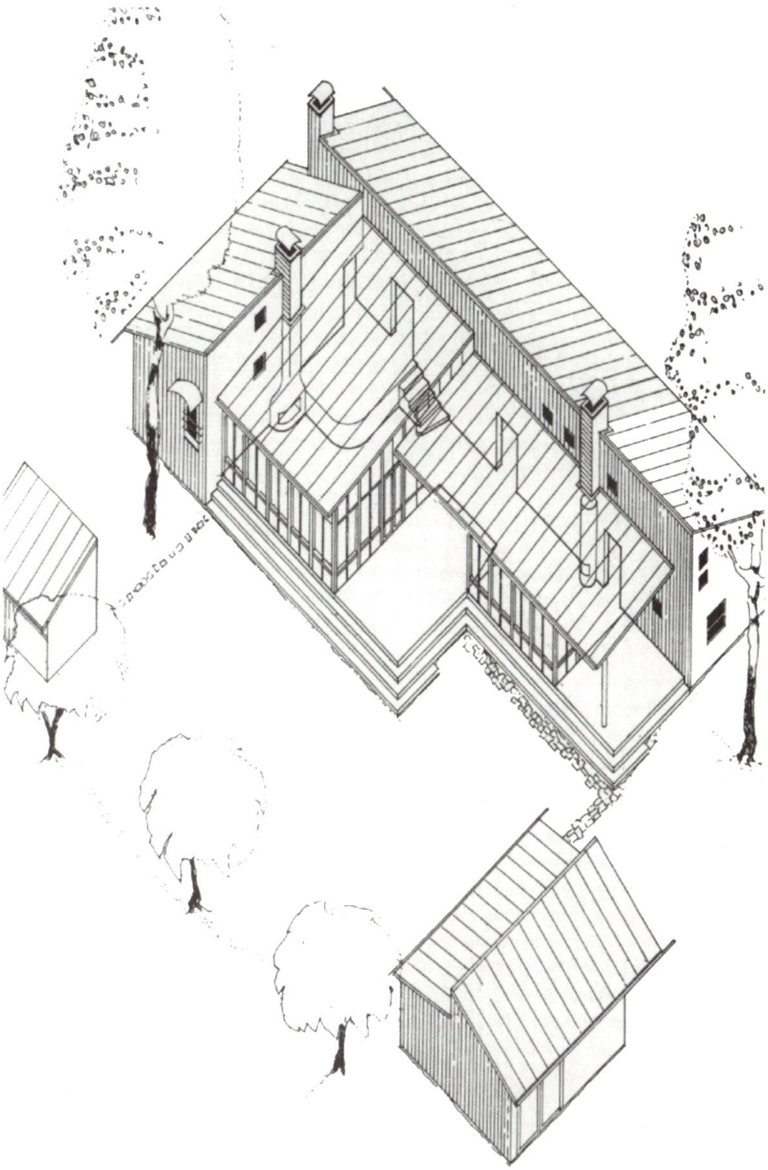

The warmth of wood creates impressive interiors. The slope of the roof adds more volume to the rooms.

Philippe Rotthier & Atlante

La Maison du Bourgmestre

Lasne, Belgium

Photographs: Yvonne Gauthier & Pia G. Cruz

For the architect Philippe Rotthier, the theory and research of vernacular architecture is a central component of building practices. Designed in conjunction with Atlante Studio (headed by architects Olivier de Mot and Jean-François Lehembre), this house for the mayor of Lasne (located not far from Brussels), drew on the traditional building techniques for houses and farms in the Wallon area of the Brabant province.

The house was sited so as to shield it from the prevailing winds and the main facades are positioned to catch the maximum amount of sunlight. These characteristics, along with the spacious courtyard, all form part of the local architectural vernacular.

The window proportions, cornice heights, masonry bond patterns, an external chimney, the southwest facade based on surveys of existing buildings, old recycled bricks and natural stone all come together to create a house that seems to have existed for countless generations.

While the exterior shows a degree of empathy concerning the surroundings, the interior is a reflection of its relation to the client (the designer's brother) and brings innovations to the concept of traditional distribution patterns. Using the mathematics of a regular layout and the freedom of an open plan, the program seeks fluid circulation routes and, in the double-height space, gentle curves, a feeling of purity and ample light enhanced by the generous use of white. The large hall, which is set adjacent to the mayor's office and serves for receptions, is paved in blue stone and features a sculptural S-shaped staircase.

This house is a successful example of reconciliation between defending the architectural heritage and the landscape with the desire for comfort and inevitable urban growth.

Set within an old orchard, the house is aligned with the rows of existing trees. A succession of rustic details greets visitors approaching the main entrance: a narrow path, a privet hedge, the courtyard with its old apple tree and stone steps.

The town of Lasne has a landscape of great beauty and is located near the battlefield of Waterloo, a protected historic site.

Ground floor plan

The house consists of two bodies. One is a longitudinal body with two levels of moderate height (less than 16 feet to the cornice). Set perpendicular to this main volume is a second, lower body, as if it were a farmhouse annexed to the main building. This volume houses the main living area with a mezzanine.

First floor plan

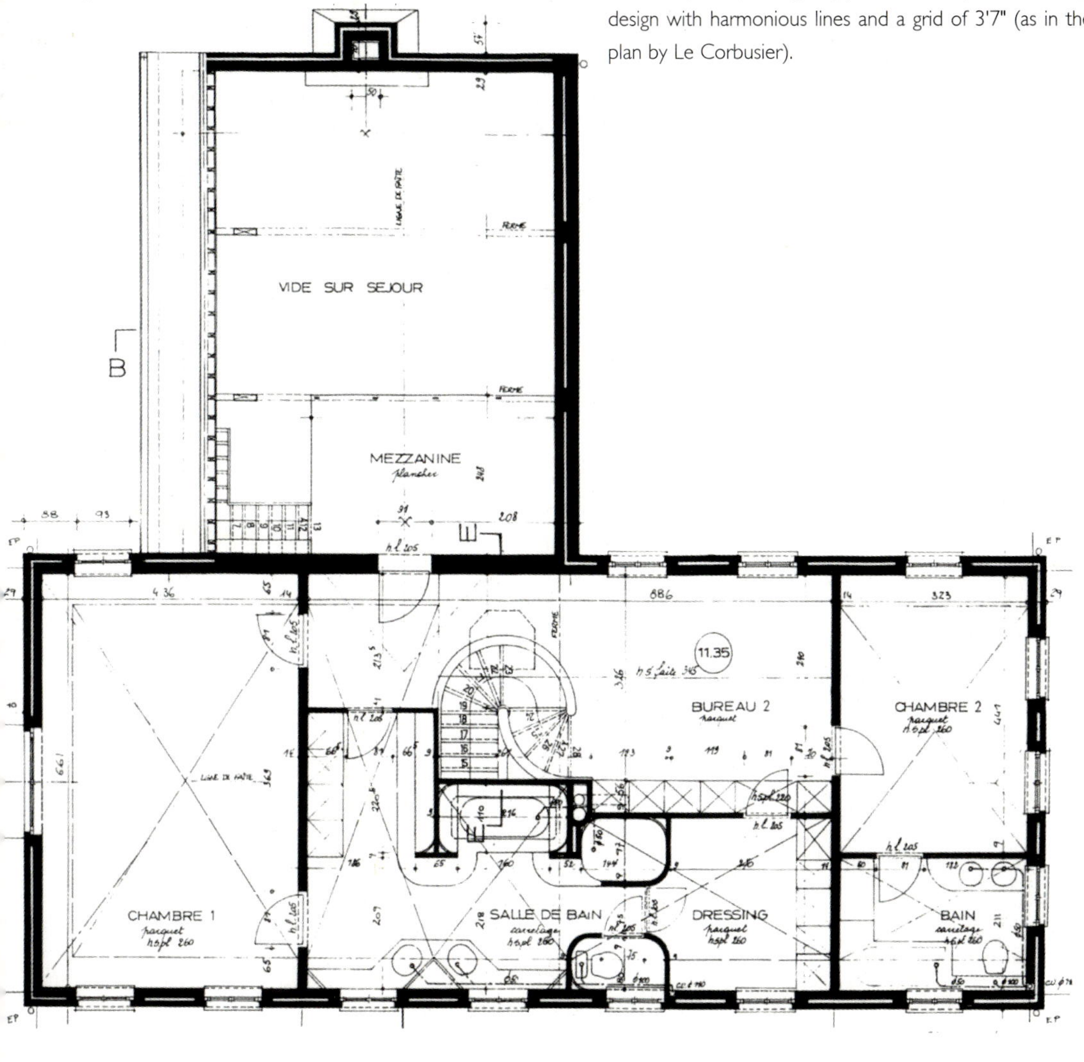

The compositional logic appears in the plans of the preliminary design with harmonious lines and a grid of 3'7" (as in the modulor plan by Le Corbusier).

Section of the secondary body

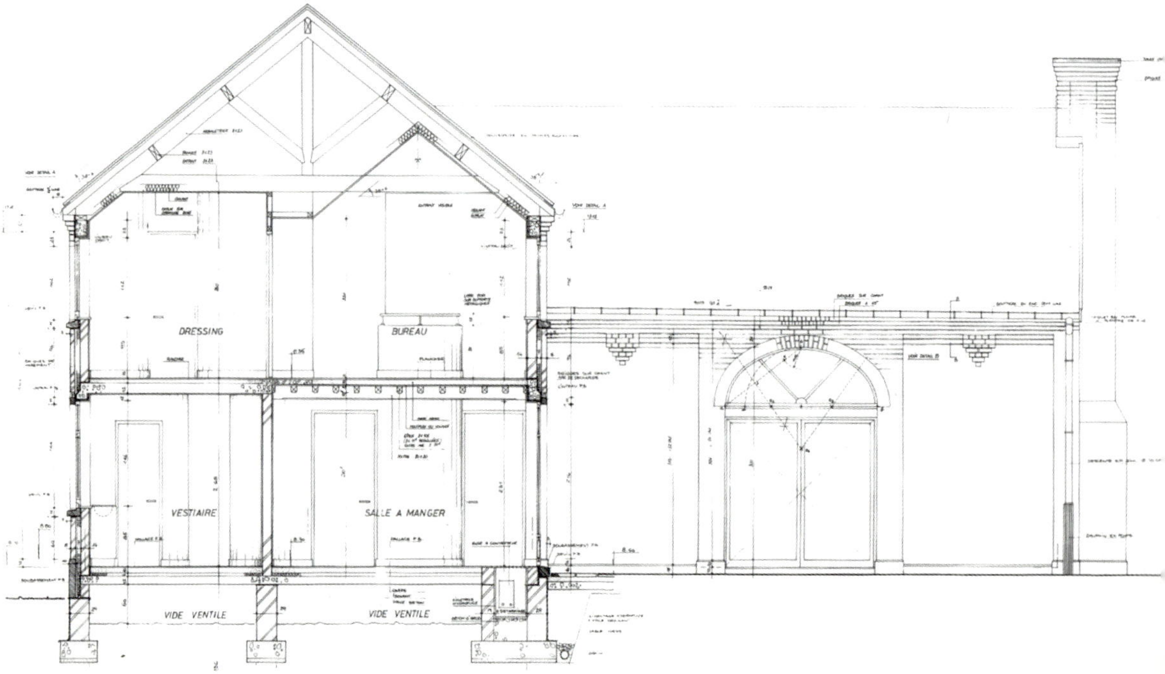

The construction work, by a small family-run firm supervised by the Atlante Studio, is of outstanding quality. Although the floors are of moderate height, the mastery of scale is appreciated in the quality of the house.

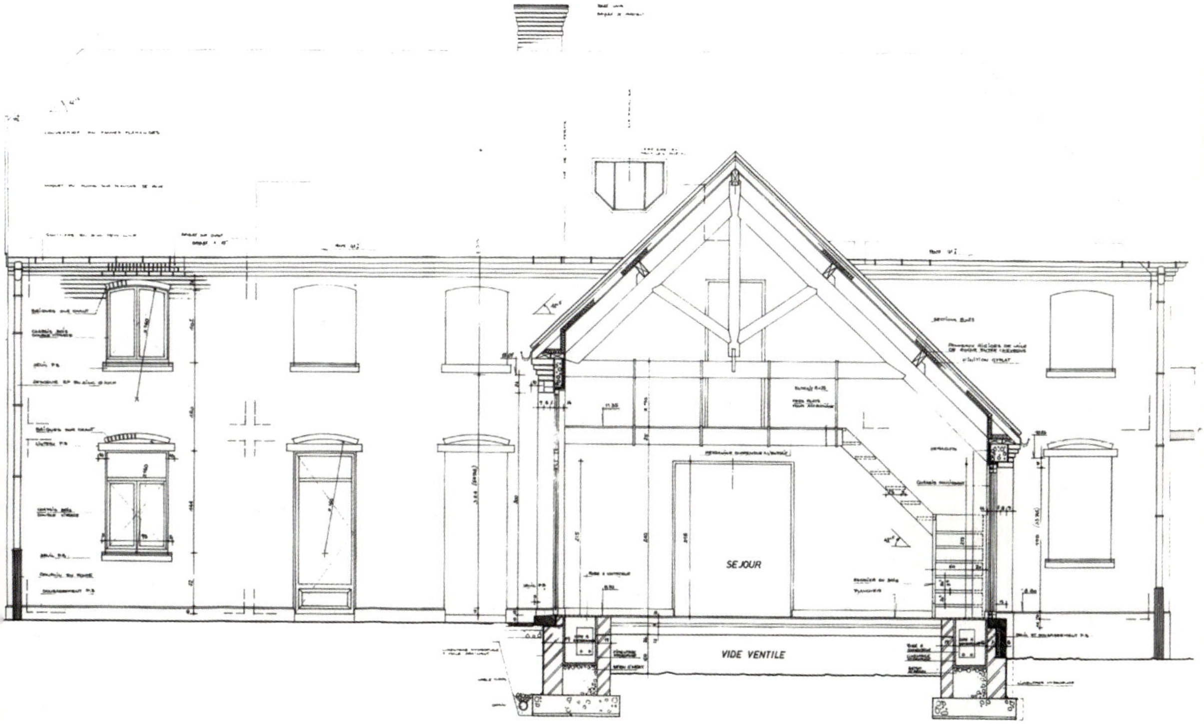

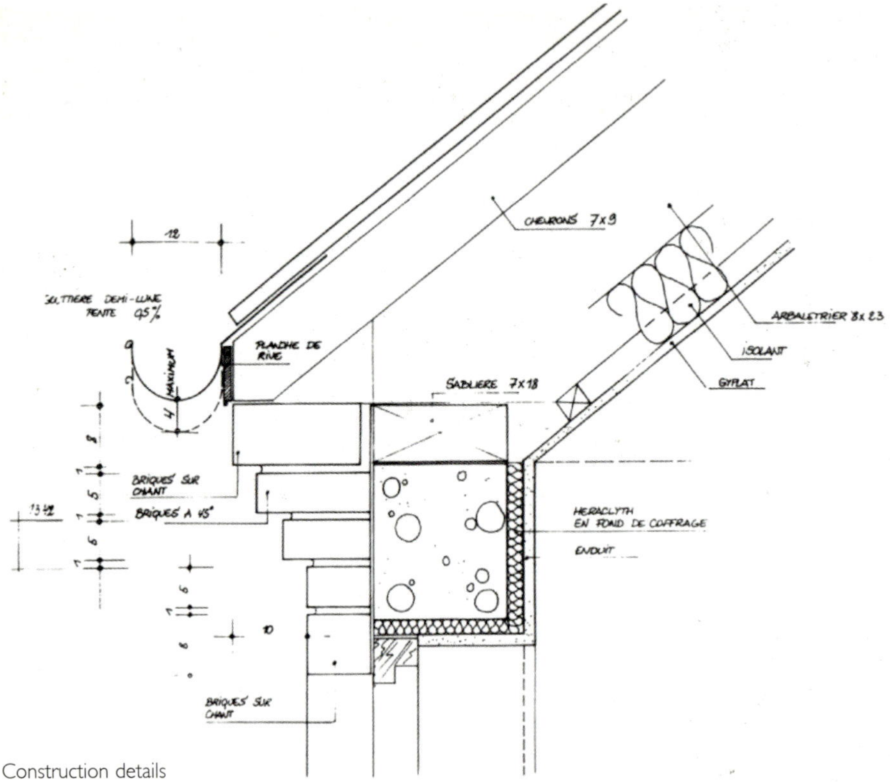

Construction details

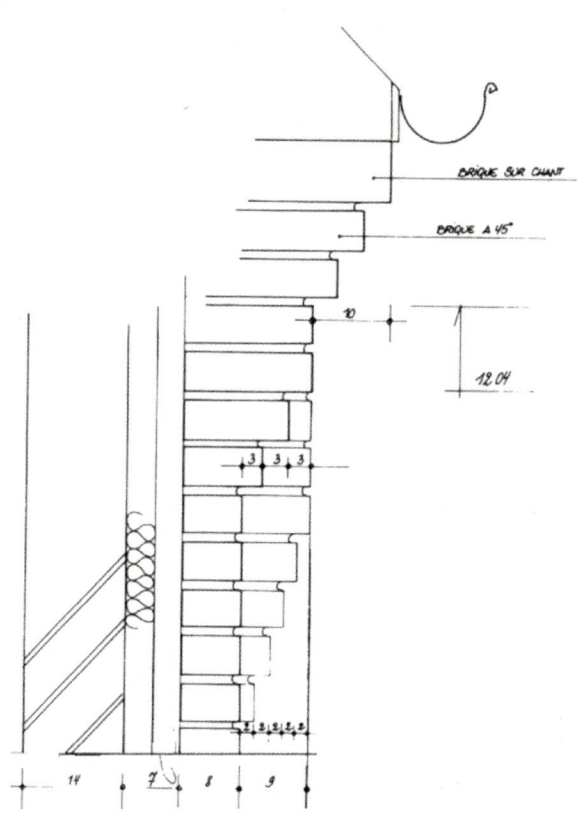

Elie Mouyal

Maison Defourcault

Marrakech, Marocco

Photographs: Elie Mouyal

Following the millennial tradition of his country, Elie Mouyal uses adobe construction techniques. The almost exclusive use of this material for the walls, floor, arches and roofs (vaulted and domed) gives great coherence to his projects. They are the fnely crafted results of a concept based on strict geometric order.

Located not far from Marrakech, the Dufourcault house is set primarily along an east-west axis between the property's two rows of olive trees.

A path raised just above ground level, as in the tradition of the gardens in the Maghrib, leads to the entrance.

An outstanding feature of the house is the external staircase leading to the terraces that form the roofs of the building and to a sort of small belvedere. In the composition of the floor plan, this element marks a clear separation between the large living room and the rest of the dwelling. The circulation routes, kitchen, bedrooms and bathrooms are set to the left of the staircase and to the right is the living room.

All ceilings, which feature different types of vaults, have been made using traditional methods in adobe brick. The structural arabesques of the large living room depict a palm tree; and as the room opens on three sides onto terraces with pergolas, an interdependence is created between the exterior and interior spaces.

On the south side, the terrace forms a large external loggia that enjoys a panoramic view. Because of its vital and symbolic value, water is a primordial element of the house and garden, as seen in the pond that paints a refreshing picture from the living room, the delightful design of the bathrooms and the long pond with its pavilion, a refined ornament of the garden.

The staircase that leads to the terraces and ends with a sort of belvedere is an important feature on the north and south facades.

True to Moroccan architectural tradition, there is a very complementary link between the house and the garden, which provides harmony through its rhythm and color.

A succession of spaces (living room, central courtyard, pond) is set along a central east-west axis. The details of structural elements made from adobe are subtly and simply combined with ornamental metal and wood motifs.

The water mirror (shown on the following page), the symbol of the origin of life, is viewed from the south terrace of the large living room.

Legorreta Arquitectos

Akle House

Valle Bravo, Mexico

Photographs: Lourdes Legorreta

Casa Akle is a holiday residence located near Rio Bravo. The construction is relatively small (2691 ft2), but sufficient for the clients, a young couple. The design is marked by the steep slope of the land, which led to a solution of terraced volumes.

Inspired by the local architecture, sloping roofs were used to adapt to the climatic conditions. The materials selected, mostly manufactured locally, allow for simple maintenance: stone or concrete flooring, fiberglass doors and oxide-based paint.

In these two projects, we find the recurring elements of the work of Legorreta Arquitectos, inspired by traditional Mexican architecture: a bolduse of color, texture, walls and space.

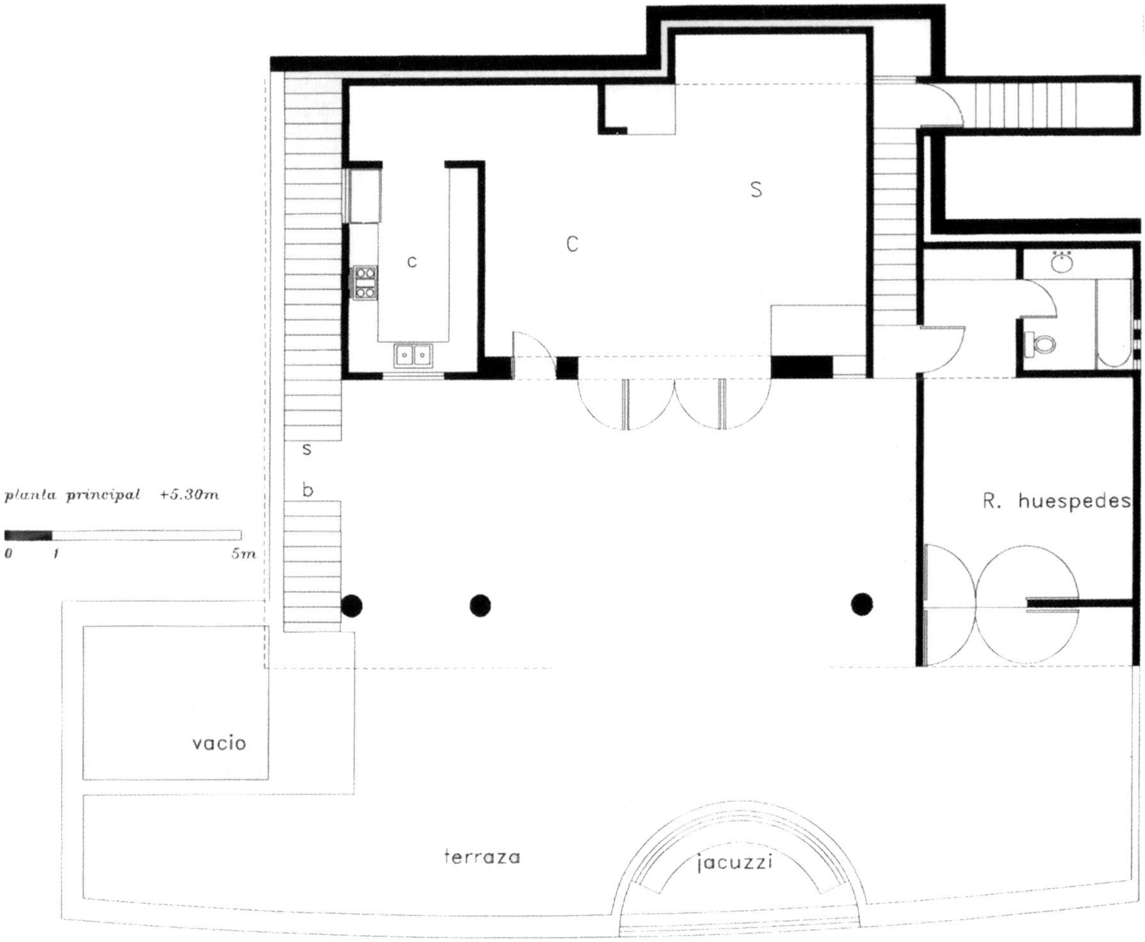

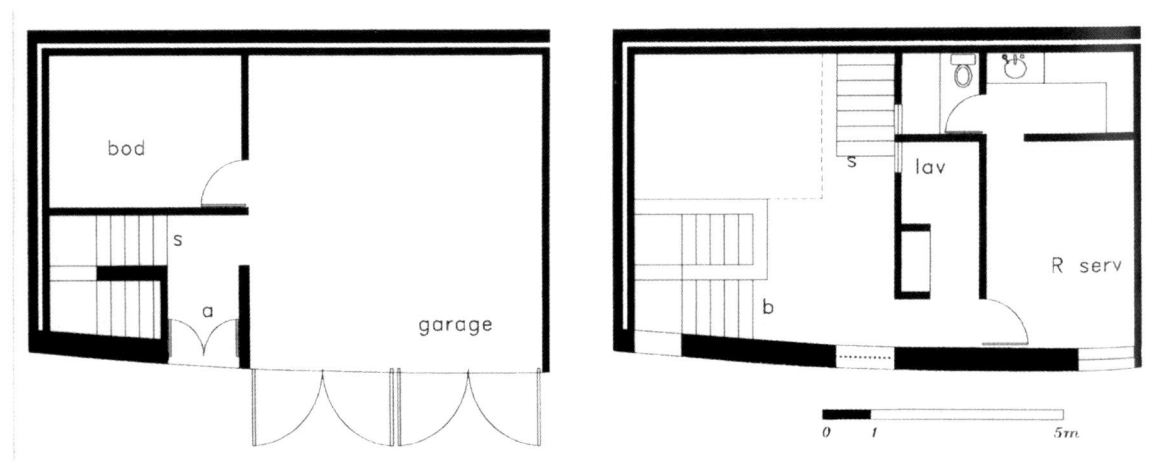

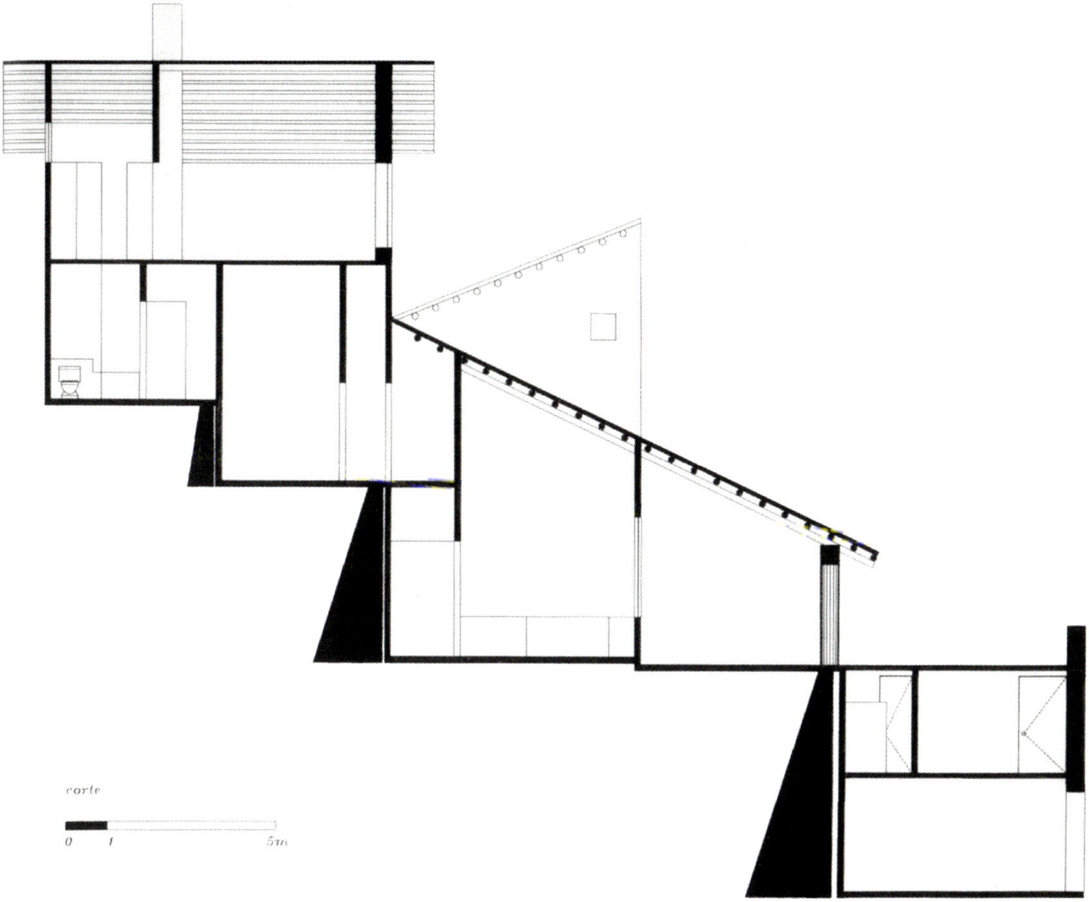

corte

0 1 5m

The plot is set on a steep slope, thereby enjoying spectacular views of the lake and the rocky pinnacle behind the house. Taking the changes in level of the natural terrain into account, large structures were avoided in the plan as far as possible.in considerazione le differenti pendenze del terreno, cercando così di evitare, nel limite del possibile, grandi strutture.

213

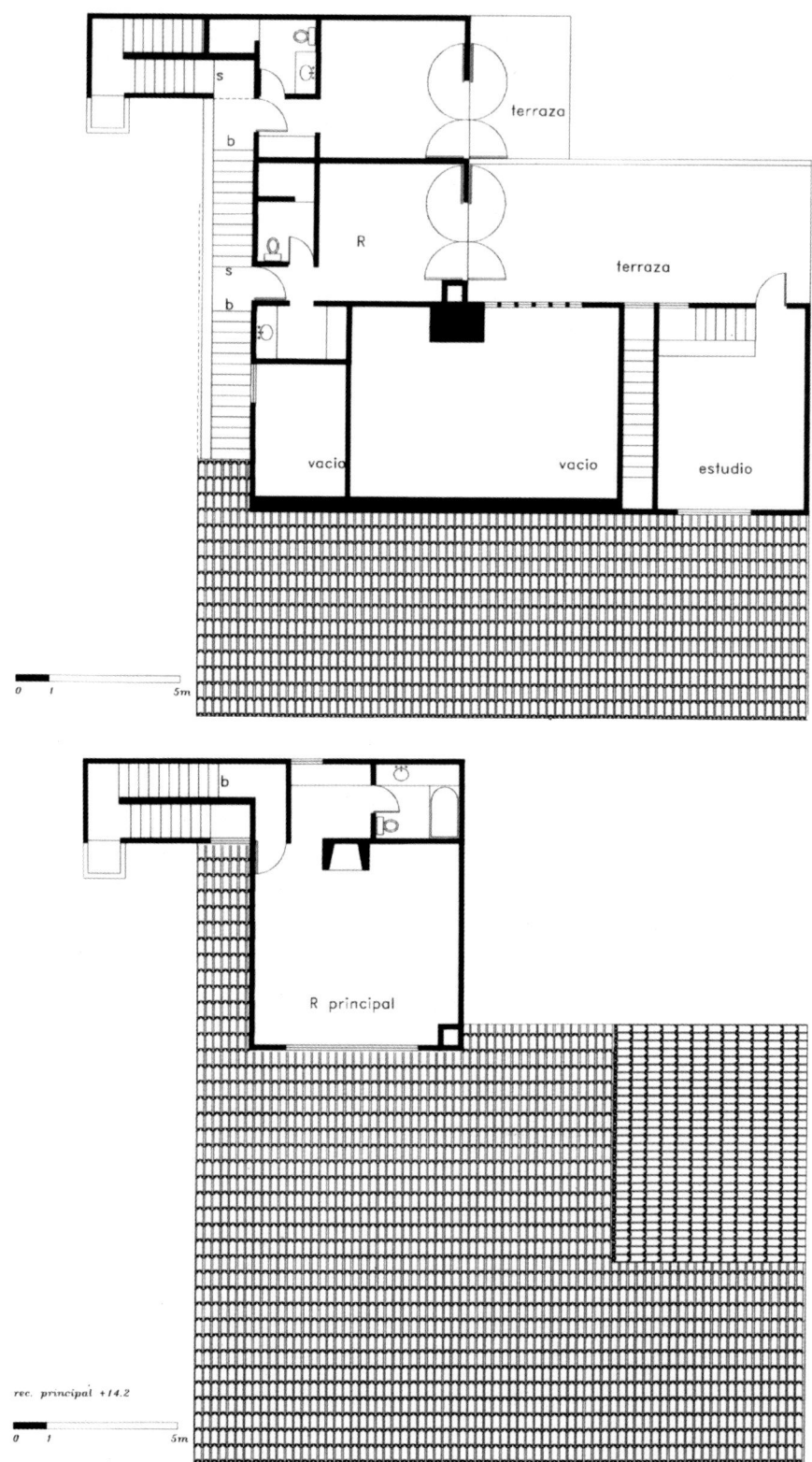

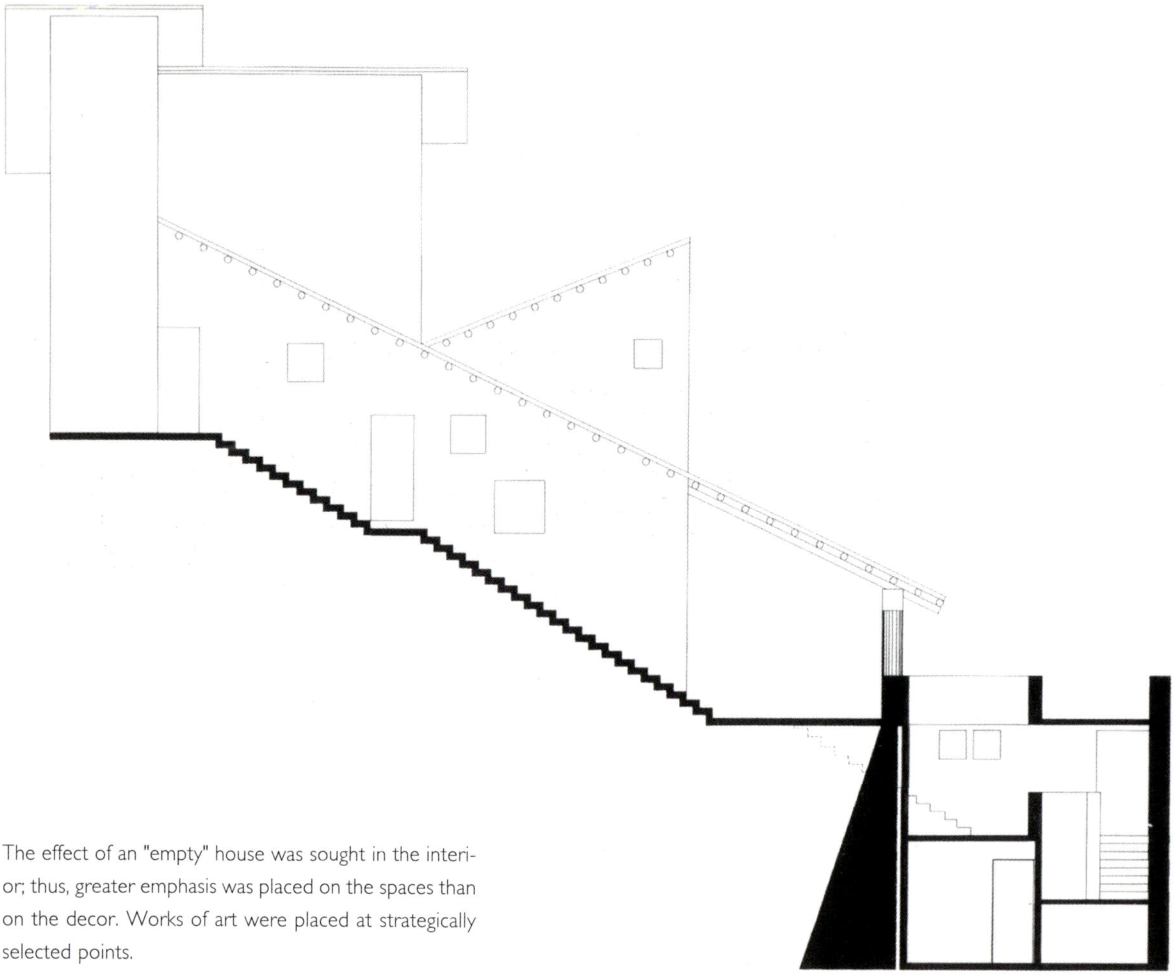

The effect of an "empty" house was sought in the interior; thus, greater emphasis was placed on the spaces than on the decor. Works of art were placed at strategically selected points.

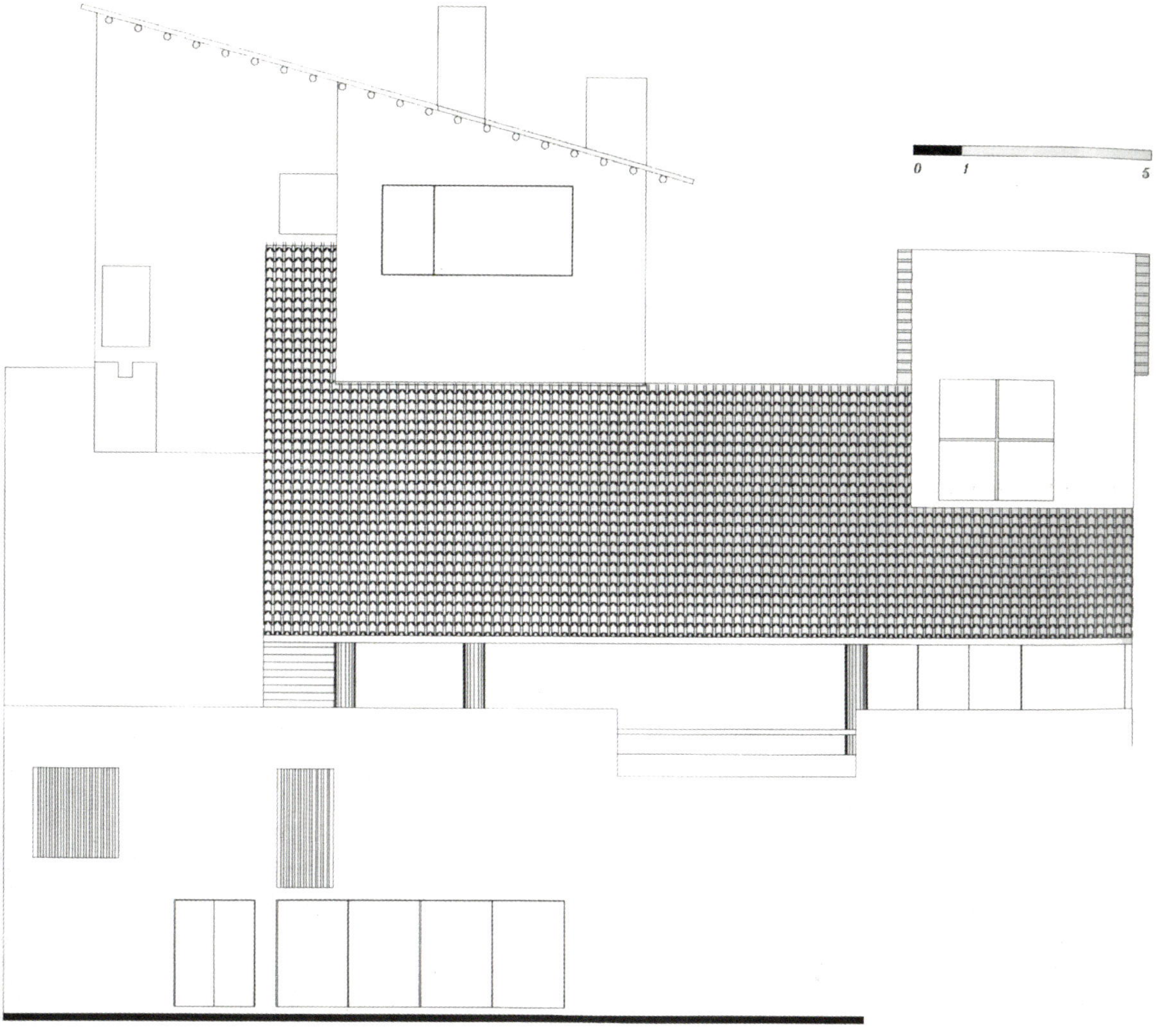

Legorreta Arquitectos

Valle Bravo House

Avándaro, Mexico

Photographs: Lourdes Legorreta

Located in Avándaro, Valle Bravo, a weekend resort two hours from Mexico City, this south-facing house was developed in the center of a 215,278 ft2 plot.

The project is structured on the basis of a private path that starts at one end of the plot, crosses a grove of lemon trees and ends in a large rotunda. This marks the beginning of a sequence of open spaces around which the house is generated, and is connected by means of a flight of steps with the water courtyard, which is itself designed as a recess prior to entering the house. Alongside this courtyard, there is also a covered walkway which serves as a boundary between the water courtyard and flower graden.

The living room, which with its sloping roof is the most important space in the house, leads into the dining room: a double-height, square space, which overlooks the flower garden and covered pool.

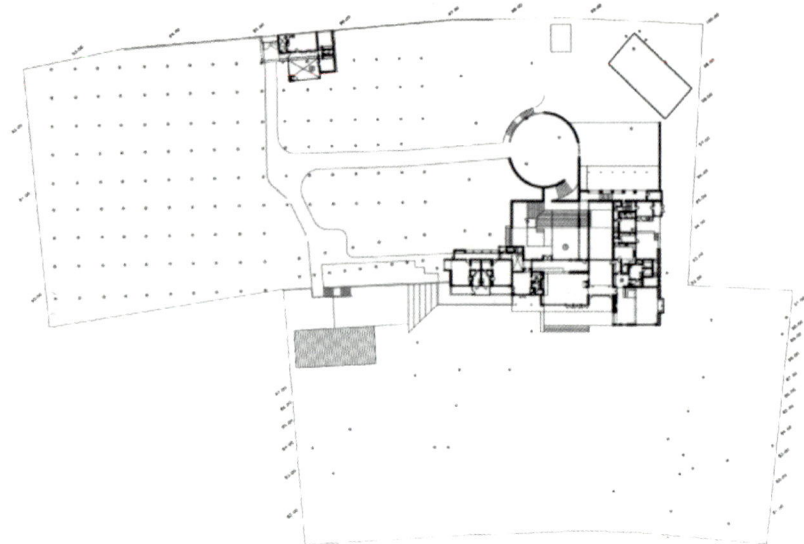

Site plan

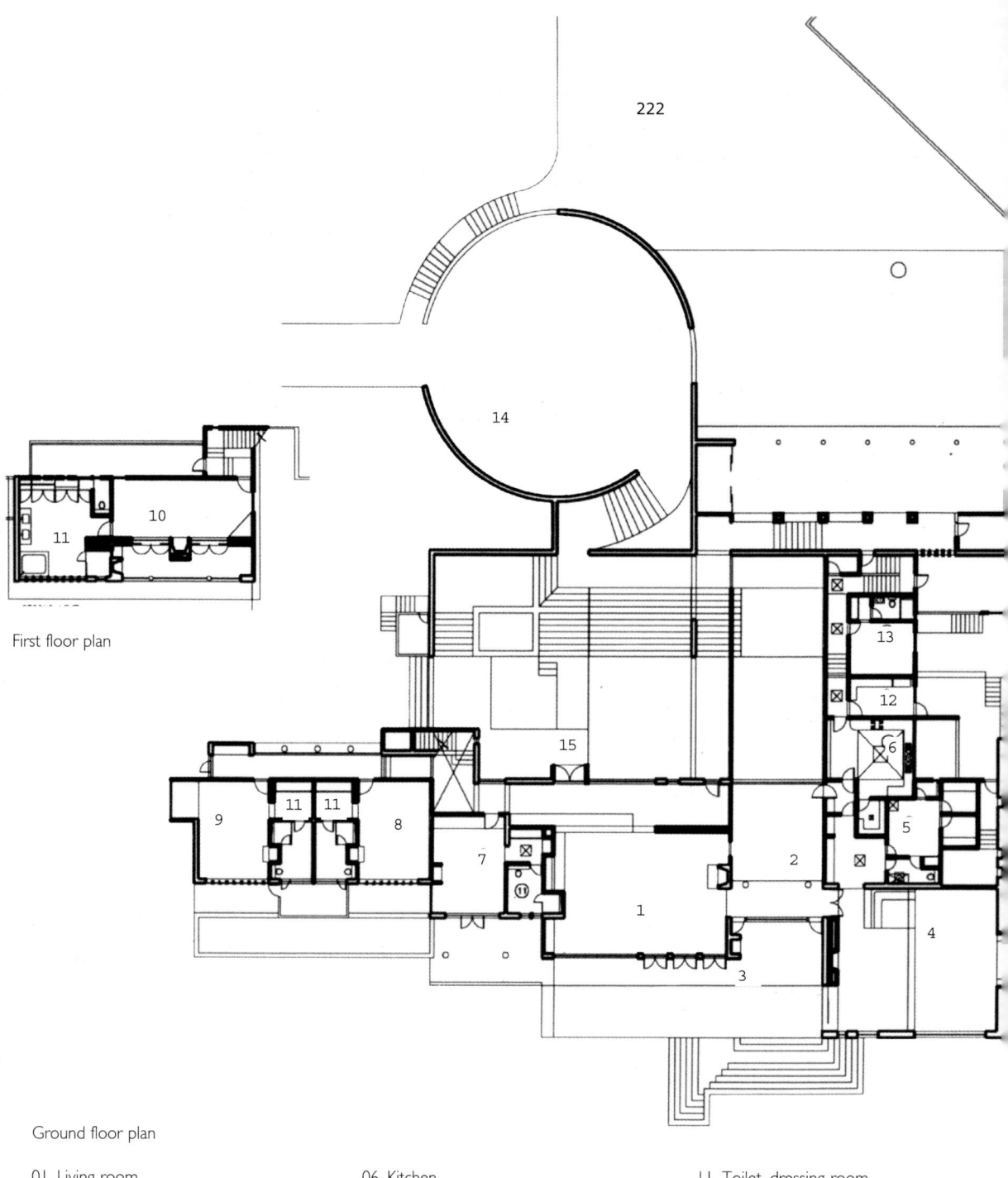

First floor plan

Ground floor plan

01. Living room
02. Dining room
03. Terrace
04. Swimming pool
05. Dressing room, swimming pool, toilet
06. Kitchen
07. Bedroom 1
08. Bedroom 2
09. Bedroom 3
10. Main bedroom
11. Toilet, dressing room
12. Utility room
13. Maid's room
14. Access courtyard
15. Access

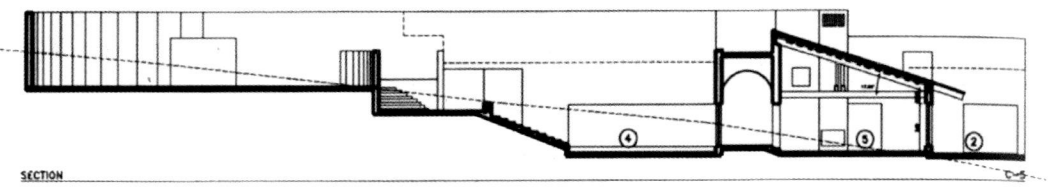
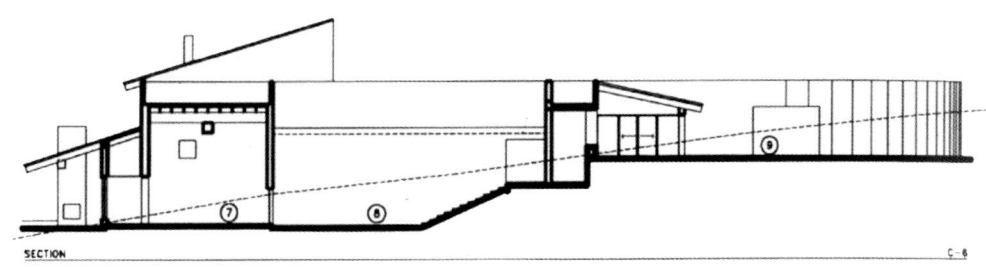
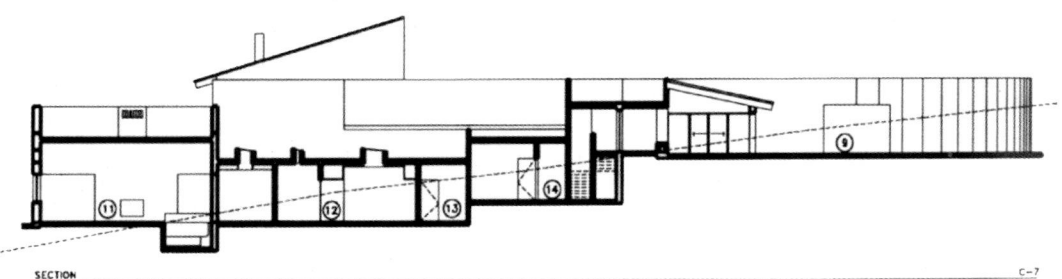
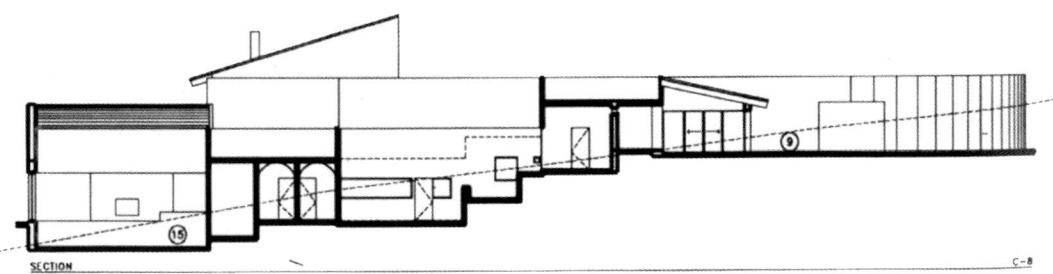

Sections

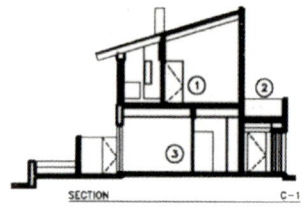
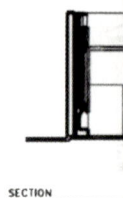
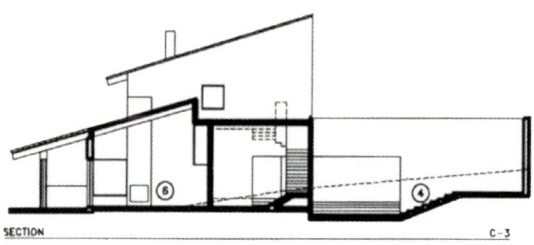
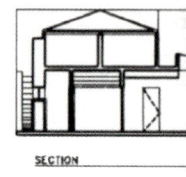
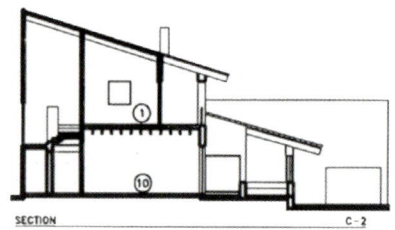
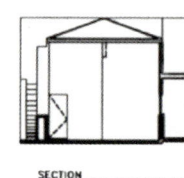
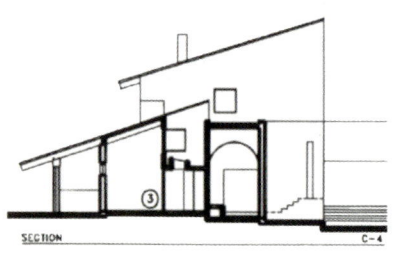

5
7
11
C-9
SECTION
C-10

1
7
16
17
18
C-11

16
C-12

0 1 2 5 10

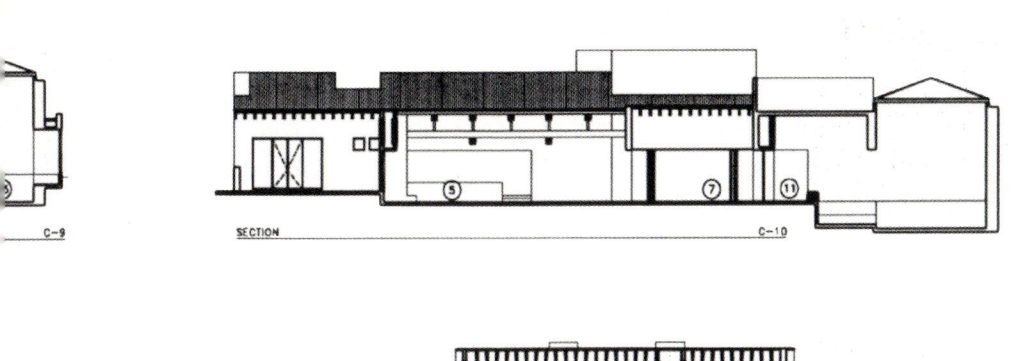

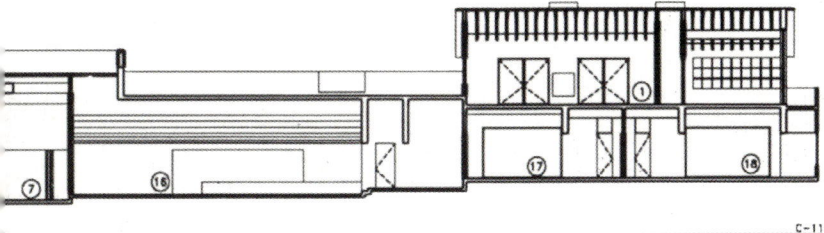

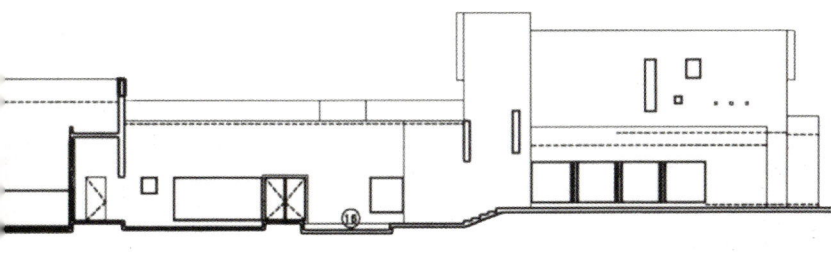

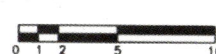

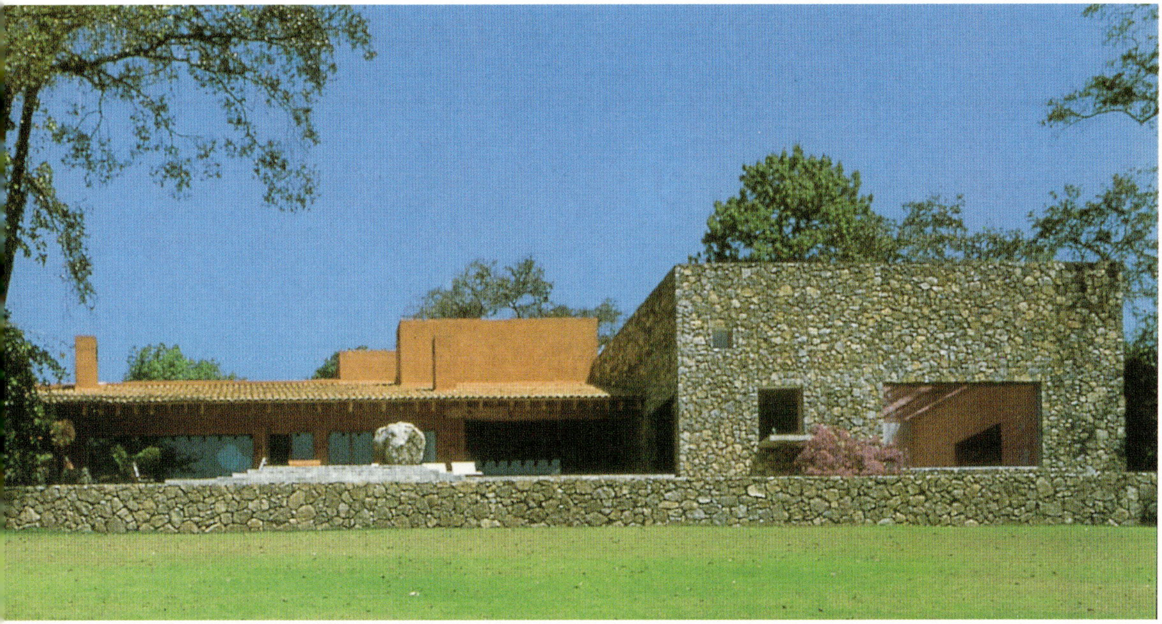

The walls of the volume in which the pool is situated are covered in stone facing, thereby providing a dramatic contrast to the rest of the house.

The house faces south in order to capture the best views of the landscape and the maximum amount of sunlight.

The house is reached via a large rotunda, which measures 59 feet in diameter and which is connected to the house by a flight of steps and the path that crosses the water courtyard as a recess before entering the house.

Maurice & Enrico Cerasi

Villazzi House

Milanino, Italy

Photographs: Andrea Martiradonna & Cerasi Studio

Villazzi House is located near Milan in one of the area's most important garden cities. Due to its designation as a protected area, an analysis of the site was undertaken before planning the design. Rather than imitating the pre-existing architectural elements of this garden city, the architects chose to reinterpret them, elaborating on a language that respects the character of this historic area.

The house's main body had to be adapted to the structure of a residence built in the 1950s. This articulation is seen in both the facades and the various levels. Unification of volumes and treatment of finishes between the new and old structures was not attempted. Light gray cement and marble powder plaster are set against cement plaster in yellow quartz paint - the smooth surface treatment of the former contrasting with the horizontal grooves of the latter.

Built in three years, the house has six levels and a surface area of more than 4305 ft2. The conservation of the corridor and wooden stairway in the center of the house prevented the creation of an interior perspective from the street to the garden and necessitated a more traditional interior distribution throughout the house. Access is gained through an entrance courtyard, which is set just below street level and covered by a pergola. The lime trees along the street tastefully accentuate the elegant neoclassical facade.

The formal result has recourse to the languages of the classical past with references to Hellenic architecture, and recalls such masters as Palladio or Schinkel, nullifying the rigor imposed by the original foundation.

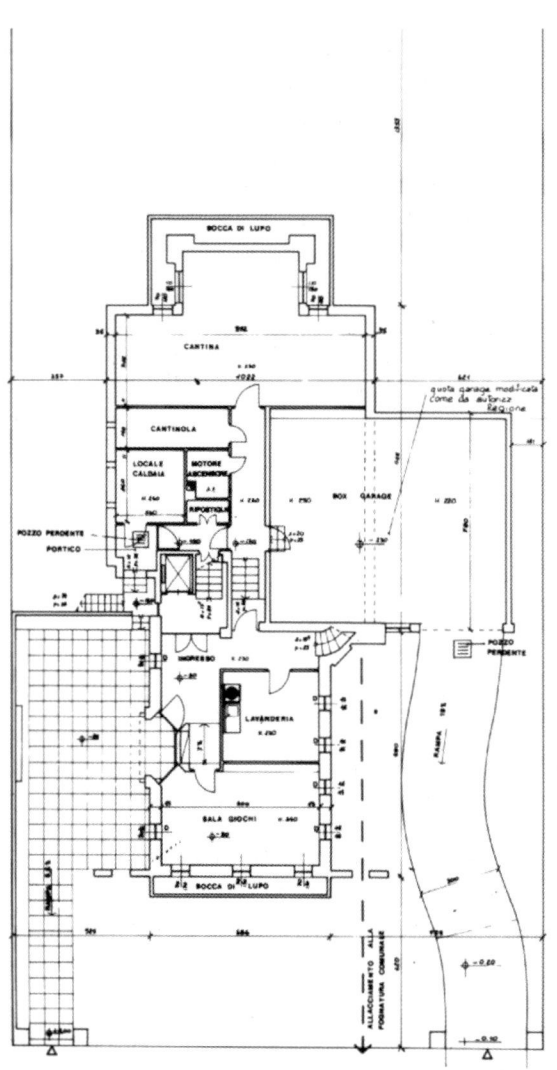

Basement floor plan

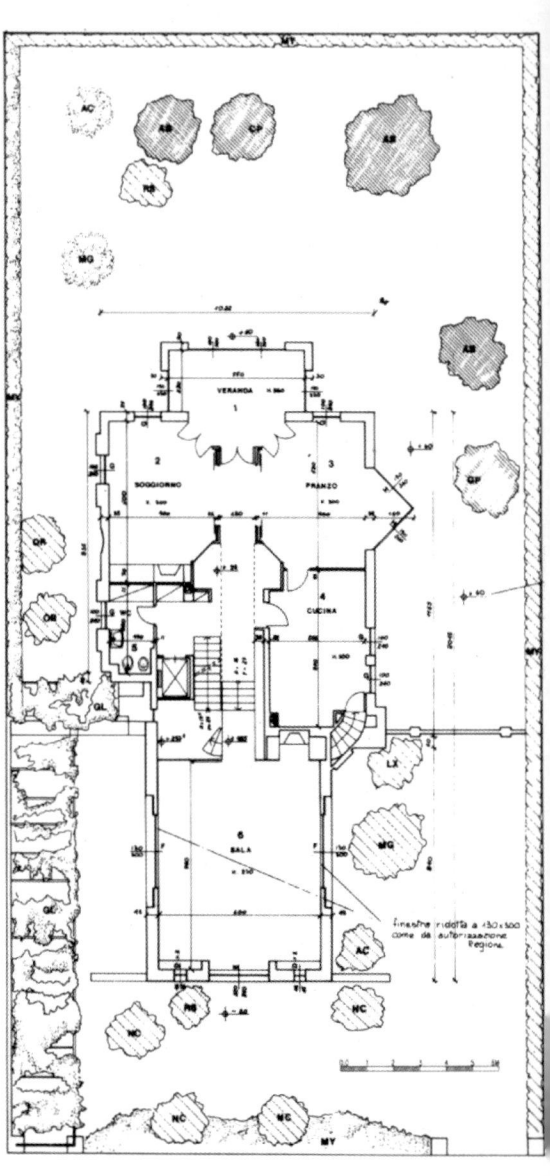

Ground floor plan

North elevation

South elevation

West elevation

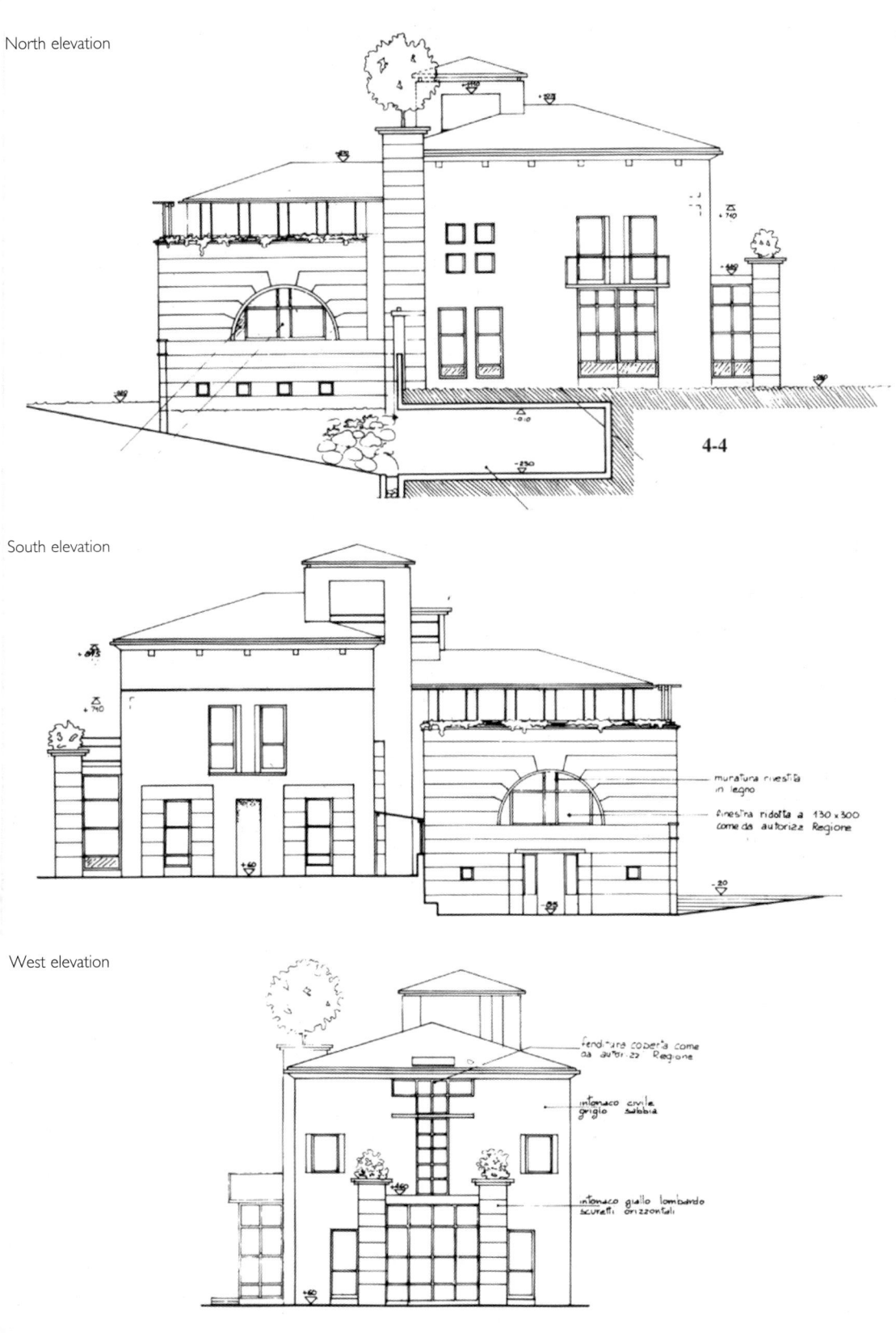

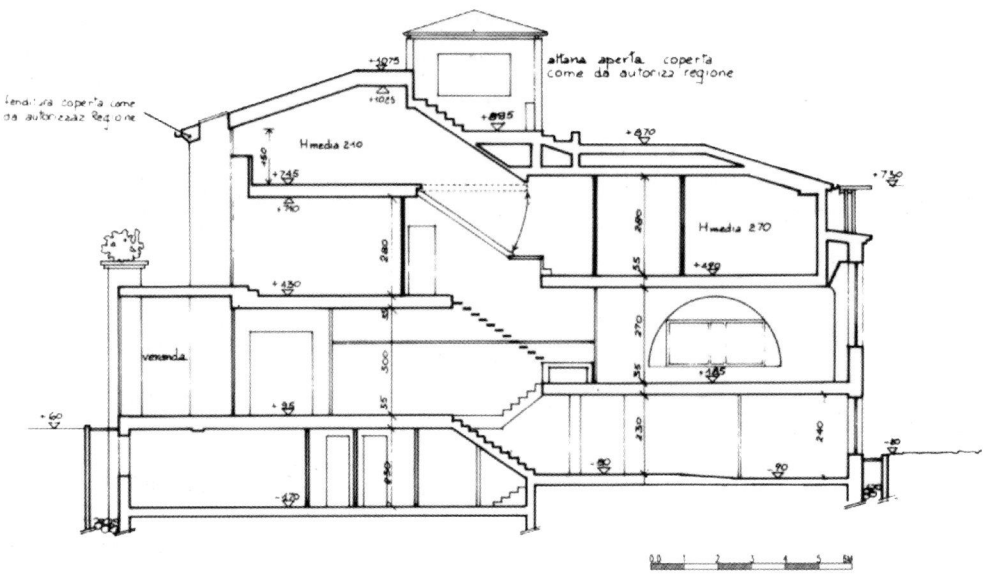

Longitudinal section

East elevation

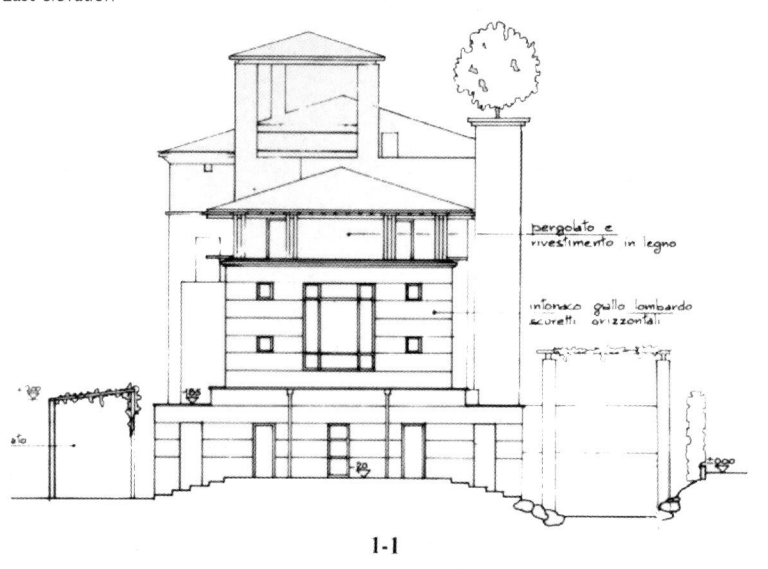
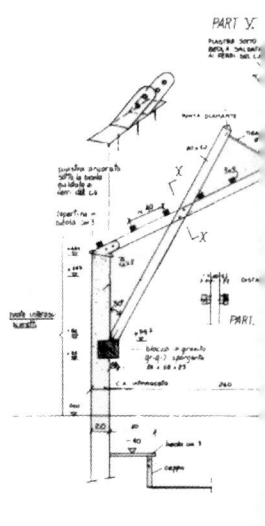

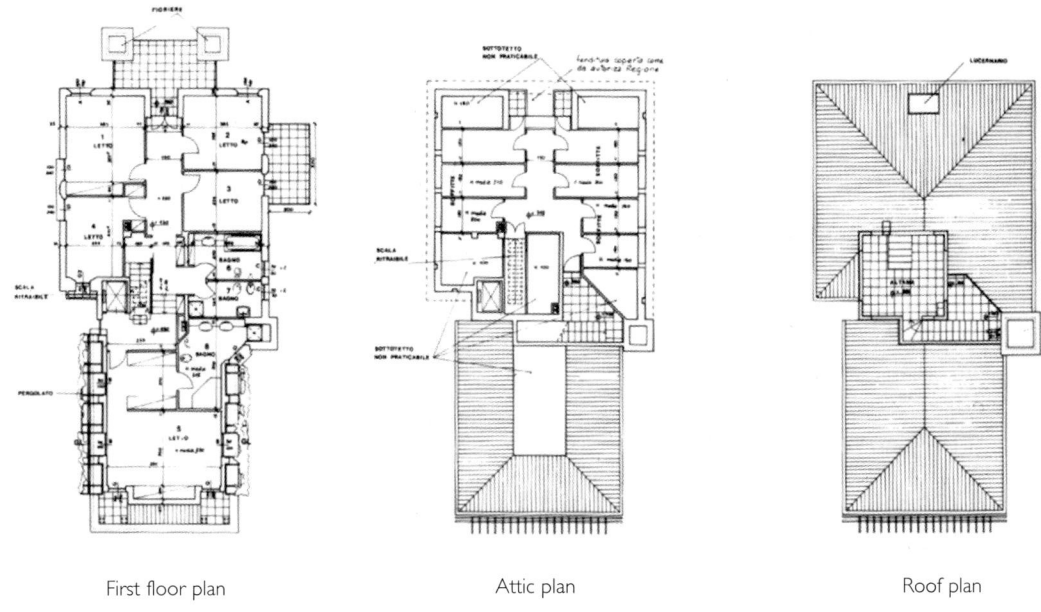

First floor plan   Attic plan   Roof plan

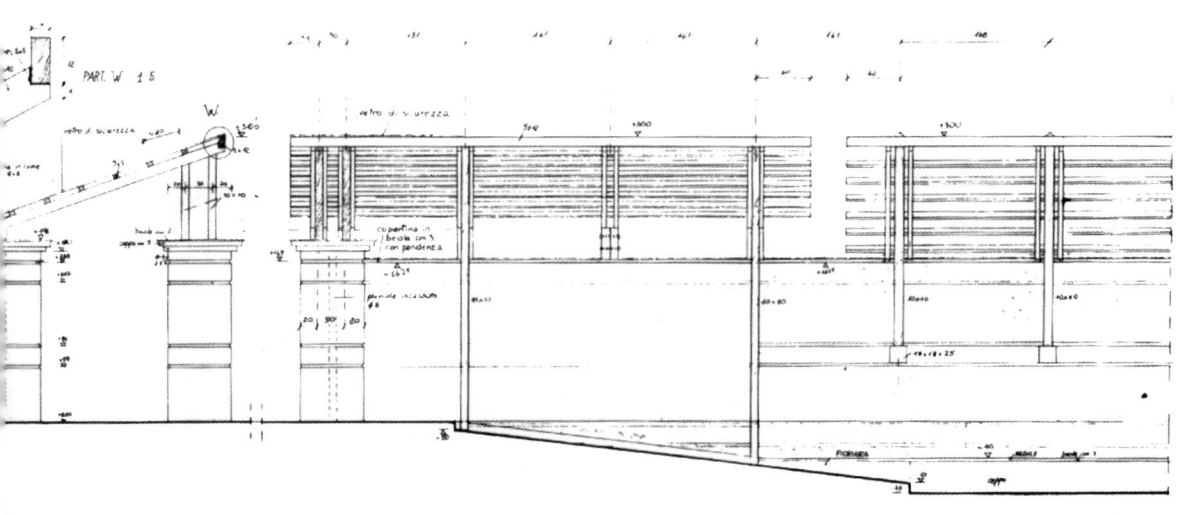

Details and finishes have been treated differently between the more public street-facing portion and the rear facade, which is somewhat plainer and more secluded.

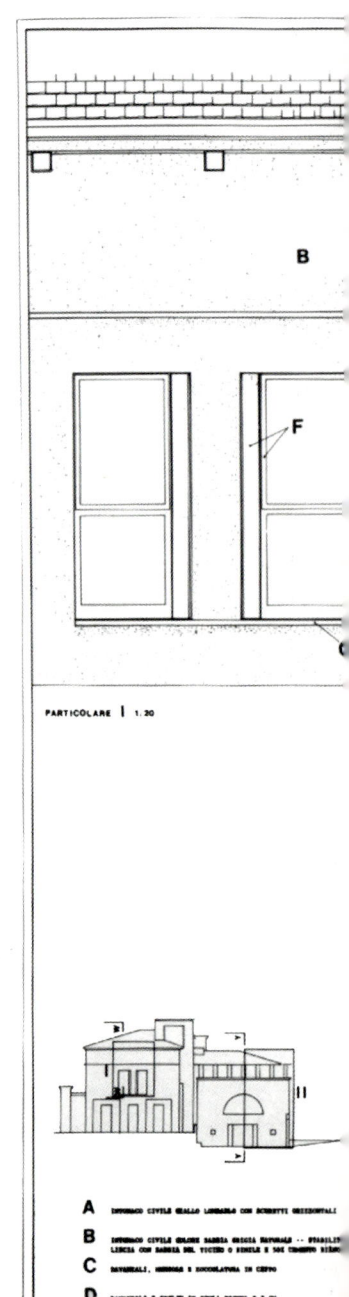

PARTICOLARE 1:20

A INTONACO CIVILE GIALLO LOMBARDO CON RIGHETTI ORIZZONTALI
B INTONACO CIVILE COLORE SABBIA GRIGIA NATURALE -- STABILITURA LISCIA CON SABBIA DEL TICINO O SIMILE E NON CEMENTO BIANCO
C DAVANZALI, GRONDA E ZOCCOLATURA IN CEPPO
D DAVANZALI E SOGLIE IN PIETRA BIANCA 2-3 CM

The windows, outer doors and roof gables are in pitch pine colored greenish blue with transparent varnish. Part of the top of the street front and gables are in marine plywood, also colored with the same varnish. The roof is clad in Portuguese tile in order to comply with local regulations.

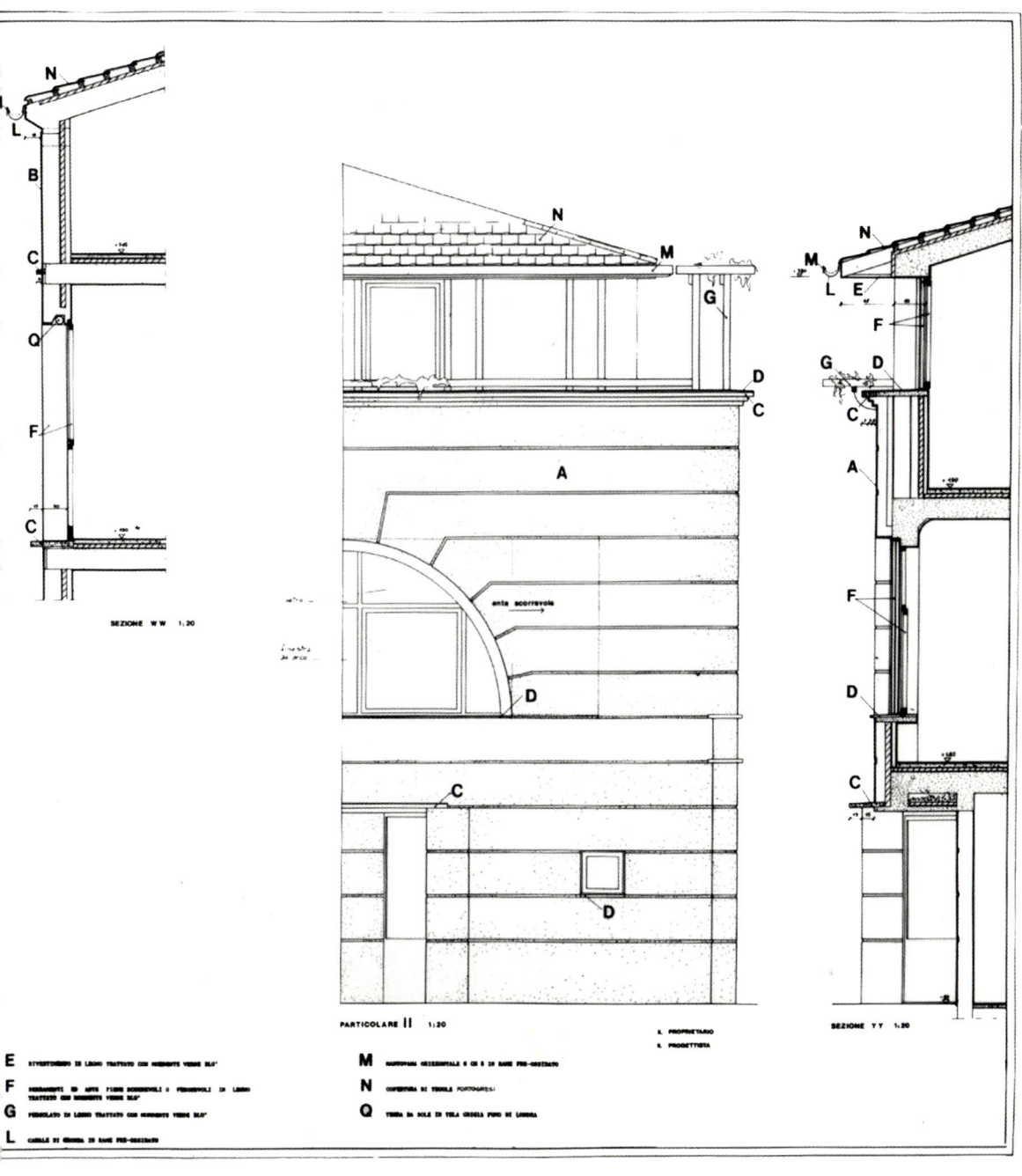

Michael Graves

Graves Residence: The Warehouse

Princeton, USA

Photographs: Michael Graves & Marek Bulaj

The home of one of the most representative figures of postmodernist architecture, Michael Graves, is a converted warehouse, built in 1926 by Italian stonemasons who built several masonry buildings at Princeton University. It was built in a typical Tuscan vernacular style using hollow clay tiles, bricks and stucco. The L-shaped building, originally divided into many storage cells, was renovated in stages.

The north wing is entered through an external courtyard that was once a truck-loading bay, and includes a living room, a dining room and a long, narrow, overwhelmingly tall library with a garden terrace on the ground floor, and a master bedroom and study on the first floor. The architect retained the original concrete flooring, treating it, however, to resemble stone.

The use of daylight throughout the house deliberately reinforces the understanding of particular rooms and suggests continuity between the building and the surrounding natural landscape. Rather than flooding the house with the diffuse light of the outdoors, Graves' more selective approach has the effect of energizing the interiors with a dynamic sense of the time of day and year.

The house is carefully furnished with an extensive collection of books, objects, furniture and art, creating convivial settings that convey a sense of inhabitation and reinforce the feeling of domesticity. The exterior pink stucco, the interior decoration, the niches and columns, all enhance the classical inspiration of the original building.

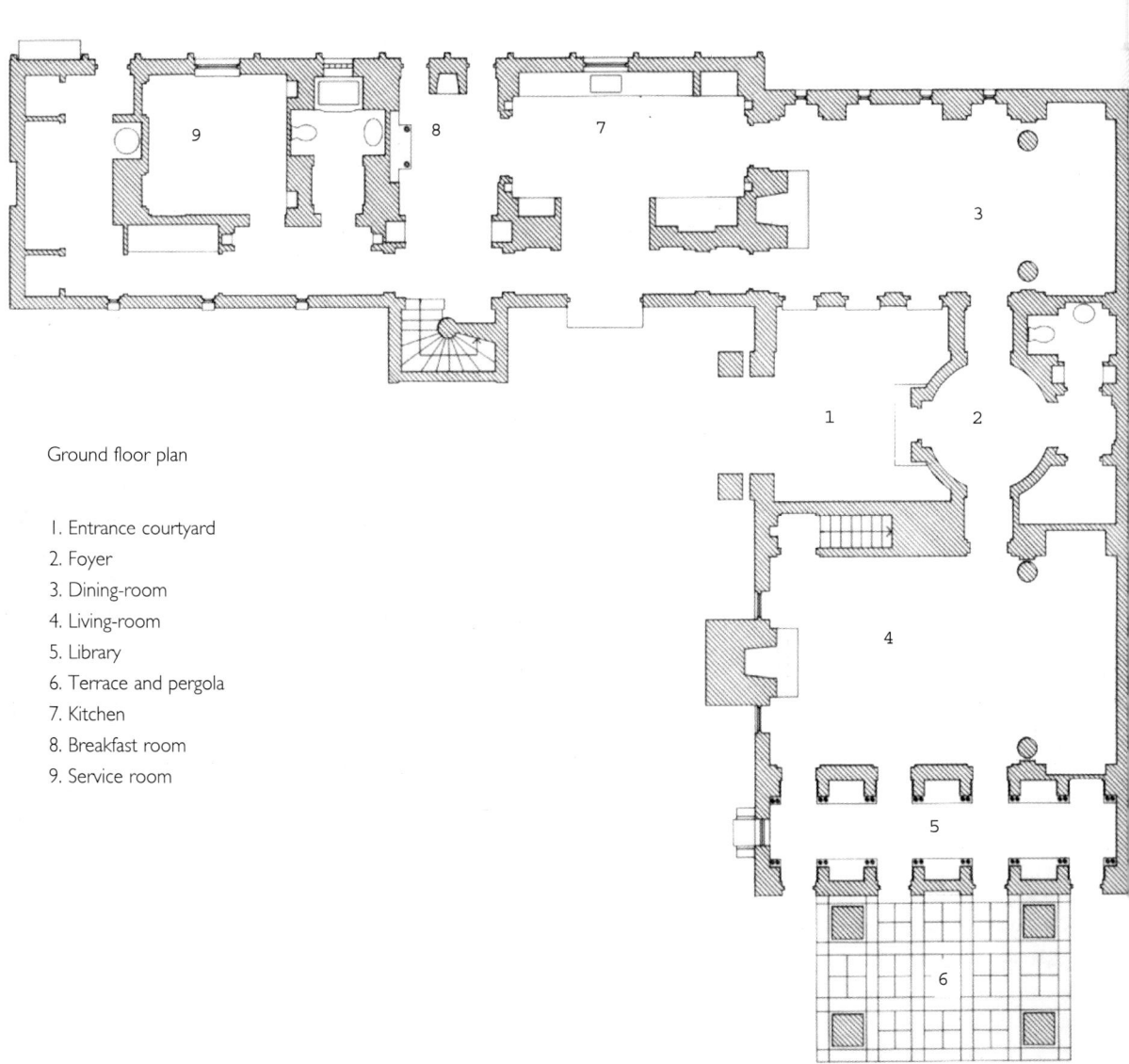

Ground floor plan

1. Entrance courtyard
2. Foyer
3. Dining-room
4. Living-room
5. Library
6. Terrace and pergola
7. Kitchen
8. Breakfast room
9. Service room

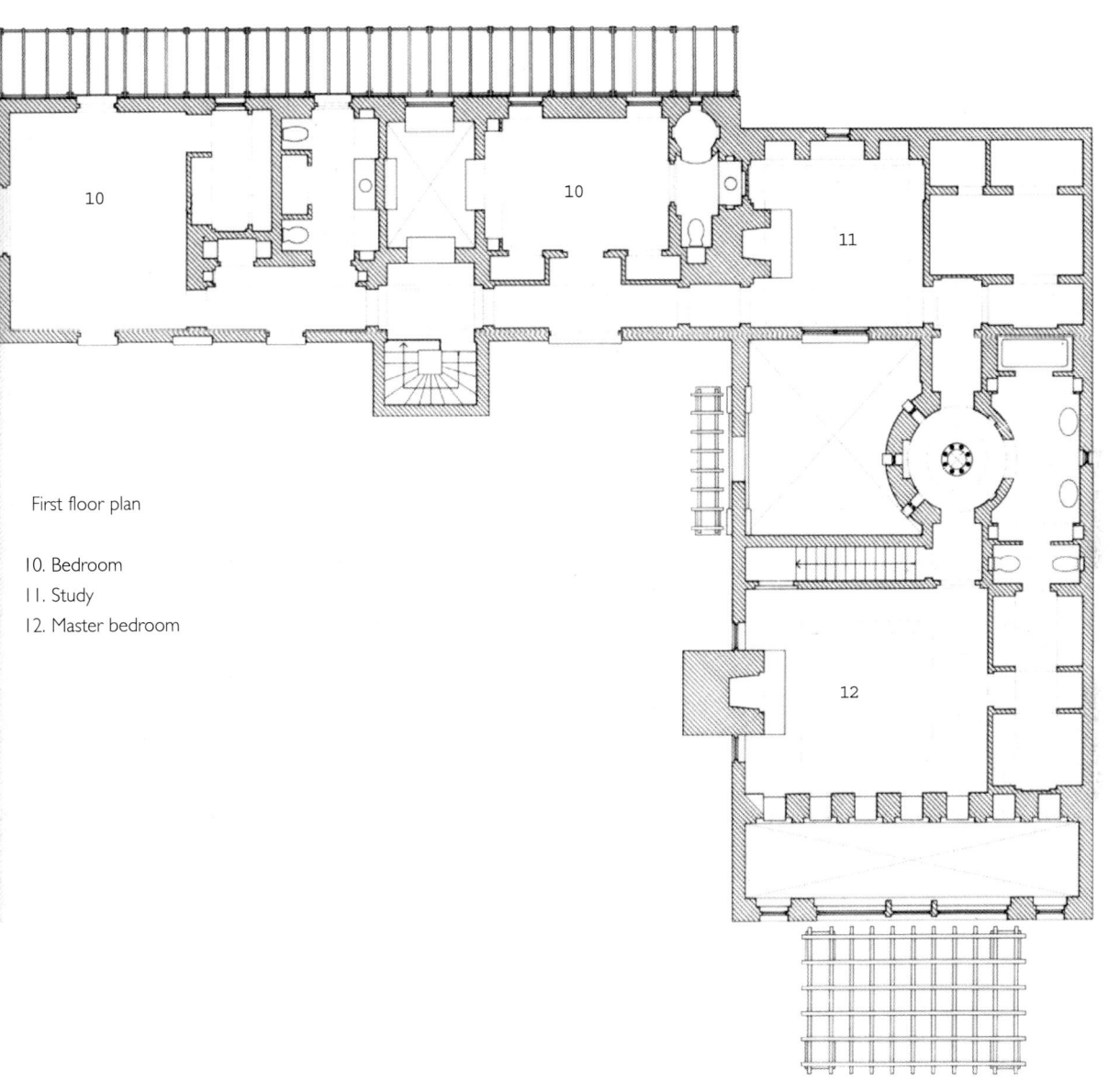

First floor plan

10. Bedroom
11. Study
12. Master bedroom

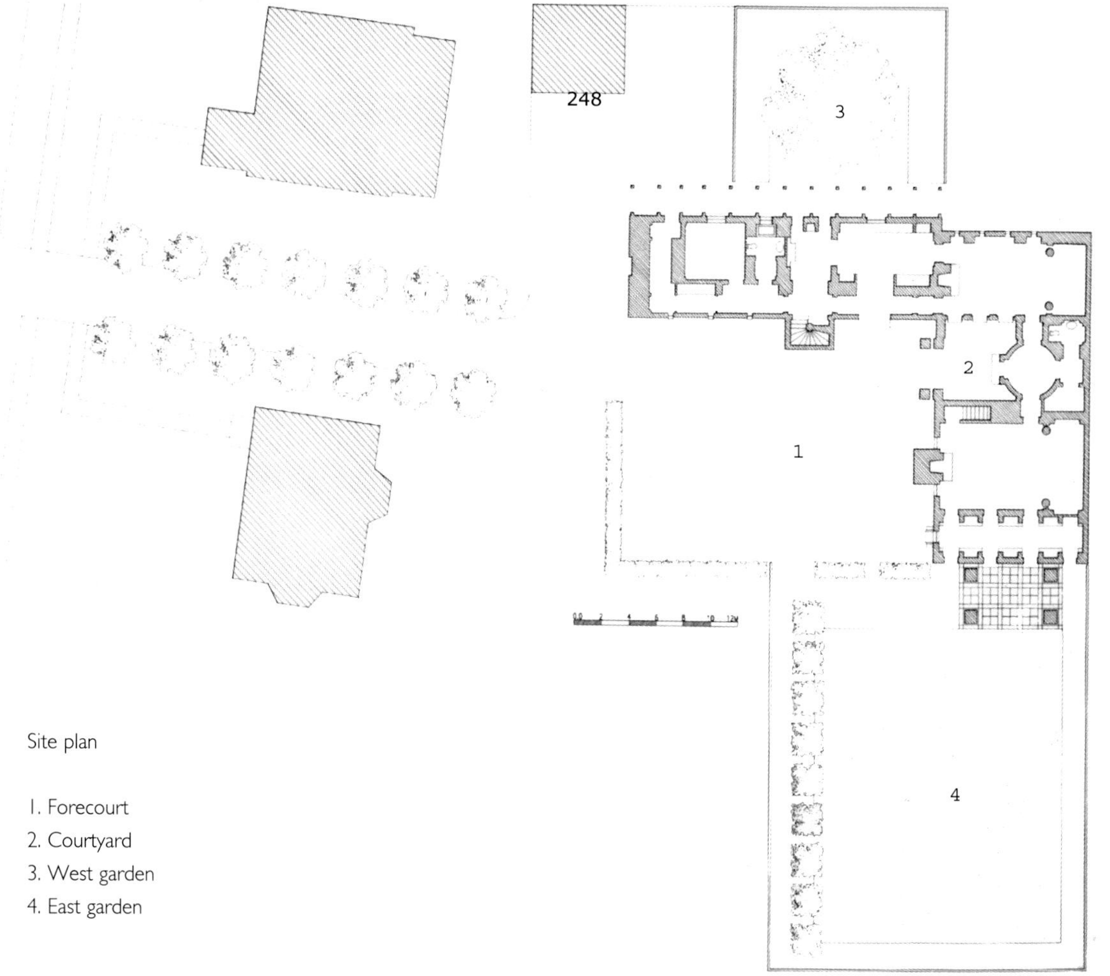

Site plan

1. Forecourt
2. Courtyard
3. West garden
4. East garden

East-west section of north wing

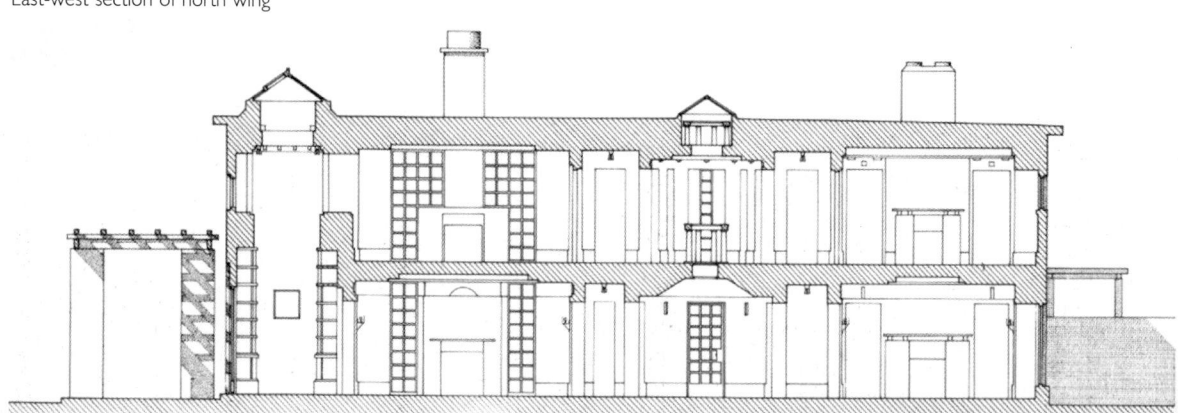

North-south section through west wing and north wing

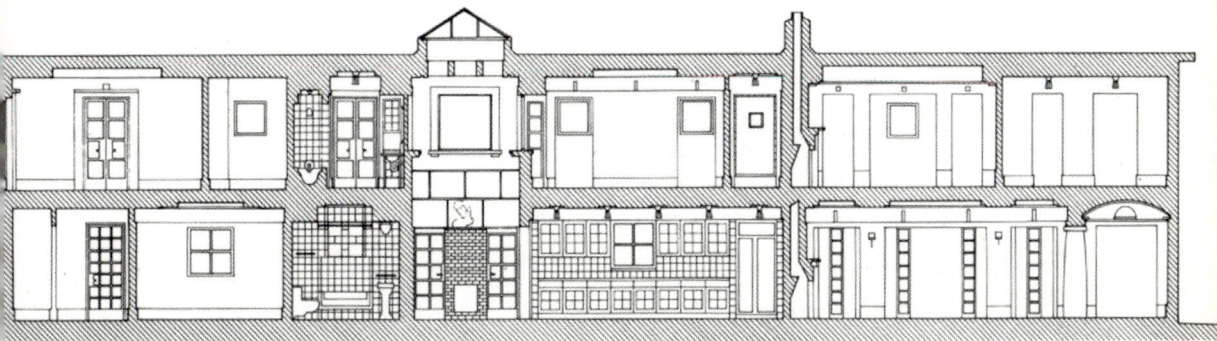

North wing, section through entry, courtyard and foyer.

The library occupies a place of honor in the Warehouse project, facing the principal garden. Privacy is preserved and light filtrated by the glycine of a massive pergola.